S0-AIY-423

BELGIAN
ADMINISTRATION
IN THE CONGO

GEORGES BRAUSCH

LIBRARY
College of St. Francis
JOLIET, ILL.

Issued under the auspices of the
Institute of Race Relations, London

OXFORD UNIVERSITY PRESS
LONDON   NEW YORK   CAPE TOWN
1961

Oxford University Press, Amen House, London, E.C.4.

GLASGOW   NEW YORK   TORONTO   MELBOURNE   WELLINGTON
BOMBAY   CALCUTTA   MADRAS   KARACHI   LAHORE   DACCA
CAPE   TOWN   SALISBURY   NAIROBI   IBADAN   ACCRA
KUALA LUMPUR   HONG KONG

© *Institute of Race Relations 1961*

Printed in Great Britain by R. J. Acford Ltd., Chichester

967.5
B825

CONTENTS

		PAGE
FOREWORD *by* PHILIP MASON		vii
INTRODUCTION		ix
I.	ECONOMIC AND SOCIAL PROGRESS . .	1
II.	RACE RELATIONS	19
III.	CONGOLESE PARTICIPATION IN GOVERNMENT	40
IV.	BREAKTHROUGH TO INDEPENDENCE . .	62
	CONCLUSION	87
	TABLE I Comparative Statistics of Non-European Students in Metropolitan Primary Schools (1956–1959)	88
	TABLE II Congolese Administrative Structure . .	89
	BIBLIOGRAPHY	90

33605

FOREWORD

THERE has been much discussion in Britain of happenings in the Congo, looked at usually from the point of view of their international importance, sometimes with a certain complacency at what seems by contrast our own success in transferring power. But there is little knowledge of the methods and problems of Belgian administrators during the years before the end of Belgian sovereignty. It is the intention of this book to throw some light on these questions.

M. Brausch is an administrator of a kind at once recognisable by a British audience. He was clearly devoted to his work; he was not always patient about control from the metropolis and was indignant that the happiness of the Congo should be at the mercy of party politics in Belgium. He is an anthropologist as well as an administrator and has, incidentally, just been appointed to a post in the faculty of anthropology in the University of the Sudan at Khartoum. In Belgian politics, as in the Congo, there can be no doubt where his sympathies lie; he does not conceal warm admiration for some Ministers of the Colonies, a lack of it for others. To some readers the assumptions which he does not state will be of almost as much interest as what he does say about the changes in policy and the reactions to them of a Belgian official on the spot.

The series of information booklets to which this book belongs is young. As it develops, it becomes clear that its books will fall into two main categories. There are those in which an outside observer, with as much objectivity as is compatible with keen interest, makes an analysis of a given situation. Gerard Mansell's *Tragedy in Algeria* is a good example of this type. Those in the second category present a point of view from within, that of someone deeply involved. It is among them that M. Brausch's book belongs. This category is no less valuable than the other.

PHILIP MASON

INTRODUCTION

FOR centuries, the territories drained by the Congo River were a blank space on the map of the African continent. They came suddenly into the public eye at the beginning of the twentieth century (1903), with the publication of Roger Casement's report on the conditions under which the rubber trade was conducted in the Upper Congo. But as soon as its news value had died down, the Congo again ...tioned for more than ... the Congo played a ...ole and its copper, ...lly its uranium were ... cause. Consequently ...rica which had made ... to be regarded with ... feeling of sympathy ...st, attracting many ... to discover in the ...zzling coexistence of ... industrial develop-

... not a problem!' 'A ... happy, although in ...ionalistic and racial ...se in Africa do the ... of living!' 'No slums ... in the middle of an ...re some of the most ...s written by foreign ...American newspapers ... 1956.

All that was true up to a point, and everybody throughout the world agreed that this favourable situation should be ascribed to Belgium's wise policy in Africa. His Excellency Minister Buisseret defined this policy as follows in an

JB

✓

INVENTORY 1/90

____ No shelf list card

____ Call No. should be:

____ Needs relettering

____ Mend

____ Change Call No. (to avoid duplication)

____ Other

interview he gave on 2 November 1954 to a group of American journalists:

'We have temporarily postponed political reforms, as we believe that economic expansion and efforts to improve the social structure should come first. We believe that this policy is bound to create the fundamental conditions for peaceful coexistence in the framework of economic and social progress.'

International public opinion entirely approved of this policy; on 14 May 1955 Mr. T. J. Hickey wrote in a special issue of *The Statist* (London) completely devoted to a survey of the Belgian Congo:

'This is something new in world history; for the Belgian attitude to Belgium's colony is unlike the corresponding view in Britain, in France, in Portugal or in Holland. The outstanding success of it prompts the reflection that Belgium may now have a message for the other colonial powers of the latter half of the twentieth century.'

But then came the years of the lean kine: the economic recession of 1957–8, the riots of 4 January 1959 at Leopold-ville, those of 29 October 1959 at Stanleyville, the slaughter between Lulua and Luba tribesmen in the Kasai Province and Tutsi and Hutu in Rwanda-Burundi, and the subsequent political unrest throughout the whole territory, interrupted by a short period of euphoria after the Round Table Conference of January and February 1960. But a few days after Independence, the world witnessed the collapse of the whole Congolese structure. Since then, Belgium has been pointed at by most of the world as the most hypocritical of imperialist powers.

To what extent is Belgium guilty? So much emotion surrounds events in the Congo, so many interests are involved, so many adventurers have invaded the country during the last months, so many news agencies are eager to publish spectacular information, that it is difficult to take an objective view of what is happening at Stanley Pool, at the mines of Lubumbashi or at the Stanley Falls.

The heights which emotion about the Congo has reached are clearly shown by the fact that world opinion about events there revolves around one central figure, even though he is now dead—Prime Minister Patrice Lumumba, who is likely to go down in history as the African Bolívar. At present the nations of the world are divided into pro-Lumumbists and anti-Lumumbists, with very few trying to be really objective in this quarrel.

In this booklet I shall try to lay aside all emotion, to abstain from value judgments and to assess the events in the Congo in the last years impartially, according to the most rigorous scientific principles of objective investigation. Political phenomena obey laws in the same way as economic and social phenomena; my aim is to analyse scientifically the Belgian system of colonial administration in Africa during the years immediately before the end of Belgian rule, and the impact of this system on the inhabitants. Then I shall examine the extent to which the Africans shared in the economic and social progress, and in the government of the country; I shall also deal with human relations and try to point out the causes of the Congo breakdown.

In addition to the high praise indisputably deserved by the Belgians, this book contains grave criticisms, especially of the lack of competence and authority displayed by some of the highest officials in the process of decolonisation since 1958.

I hope that this study may shed some light on developments since 30 June 1960, particularly with regard to the reactions of the Congolese people to the Belgians and the other Europeans, and to the world in general.

1. ECONOMIC AND SOCIAL PROGRESS

Industrial Development

IF there is anything about the Congo on which there is instant agreement, it is certainly the economic impetus given to the country by the Belgians. With the exception of the Union of South Africa, no territory in the black sub-continent has attained such a high industrial development as the Congo, although the economy continues to include also an important agricultural sector. The Congo is a country of abundant mineral and hydro-electric resources, which became increasingly valuable from the beginning of the twentieth century, but especially after the Great War, when Minister Louis Franck was in charge of the Colonial Office (1919–1924).

In 1953 the Congo was the leading African producer of cobalt (86 per cent of the total African production), diamonds (64 per cent), tin (60 per cent), tungsten and zinc mineral (53 per cent), silver (51 per cent); the second biggest producer of copper (34 per cent) after Northern Rhodesia and an important producer of gold. The raw mineral products were as a rule treated in the country and this favoured the creation of secondary industries, which doubled their production between 1950 and 1953. Another indication of the high degree of industrialisation is given by the production of electric energy (1956: 1,743 million kilowatt hours), the highest in Africa after the Union of South Africa.

Notwithstanding this industrial development, in 1954 subsistence agriculture still constituted 80 per cent of the agricultural sector and 42 per cent of the whole local production.

The general trend of the Congolese economy between 1950 and 1954 is shown by the following figures: the value of production increased by 57 per cent, in detail as follows: agriculture 41, mining 81 and industry 100. During the same period the value of commercially-sold crops increased by 250 per cent, while the corresponding figure for subsistence agriculture was 30 per cent.[1]

In order to ensure continuity of economic development, the Belgian administration conceived a vast programme of investment, which started in 1950 and continued until 1959. When the plan was launched, it was estimated that the economy of the country could carry the burden without risk of compromising its future, since the Treasury, in addition to its ordinary abundant resources, had a reserve estimated on 30 June 1954 at more than £150 million.

Economic investment was a predominant part of the Ten Year Plan; £45 million was to be spent on roads, about £104 million on the improvement of river, lake, rail and air communications, more than £21 million on the provision of power, £16 million on water supplies. Social investment accounted for £79 million, and finally town-planning—which included housing for civil servants—came to about £54 million.

Increase in African Incomes

This great industrial development created an economic prosperity in which the African worker and even the rural population participated.

It is somewhat difficult to compare the national income figures of African countries, because of the great differences in living standards between the population groups within the country, namely between Africans and non-Africans. We possess nevertheless some indications of the growing income of the Congolese, and know for instance, according to the estimates of the 'Banque Central du Congo Belge et de Ruanda-Urundi', that the Africans' share in the national income increased from 46 per cent in 1950 to 58 per cent in 1958.[2] Although these figures seem to indicate a rather slow growth, they correspond in fact to a threefold

[1] International Labour Office, *African Labour Survey* (Geneva, 1958).
[2] International Labour Office, *Rapport sur les salaires dans la République du Congo* (Geneva, 1960), p. 12.

increase in the monetary income of the Africans between 1950 and 1954.[1]

The principal beneficiaries were of course the wage-earners, who constitute nearly a quarter of the population. The rapid improvement in the living standards of the Congolese population was confirmed by a parallel increase in consumption during the same years. Sugar, beer, cigarettes, textiles were consumed in considerably larger quantities; in the larger cities the wage-earners wanted more and more of those articles which were an exterior sign of wealth according to Western standards—radio sets, furniture, bicycles (of which there were about 800,000 in the Congo in 1960), even motor-cars.

This development was important not only from a social point of view; it was also a sign that the horizons of the Congolese consumer were being extended and that new needs were appearing, laying the foundations of a new economic development of the country through the creation of secondary industries.

The living standards of the Congolese also compared very favourably with those of neighbouring countries. The average annual income per head was estimated in 1955 at £27 in the Congo, £22 in Nigeria, £21 in Kenya, £20 in Uganda; a higher figure (£43) was mentioned for the Central African Federation. But if we deduct the incomes of the non-Africans the average African income comes to £5 for the Congo, the same for the Rhodesias, and less than £3 for Kenya.[2]

So the average Congolese undoubtedly had a higher living standard than any of his neighbours, but he did not realise this. He knew, however, because he saw it with his own eyes, that the European had a much higher standard of living than his; and the intelligent African calculated that in the Congo 1/135th of the population (the small non-African group of 100,000 people) was sharing

[1] International Labour Office, *Les problèmes du travail en Afrique* (Geneva, 1959), p. 18.

[2] *Les problèmes du travail en Afrique*, pp. 30–1.

two-fifths of the national income, while 134/135ths of the population (the large African group of thirteen and a half million people) were receiving only three-fifths. It was difficult for the Congolese to understand that such a situation is not peculiar to the Congo, but exists in many countries of the world.

Emergence of an African Middle Class

The emergence of an African middle class, including such people as building contractors, tradesmen, craftsmen, small manufacturers, market-gardeners, fishermen, transport contractors, bar-keepers and various kinds of middle-man, was another token of the economic expansion of the fifties. They remained unorganised for some time, but became increasingly aware of their importance. So when Minister Buisseret, taking up his duties in May 1954, stated that he was willing to give them his support, on condition that they organised themselves, they created, less than two months later (on 4 July 1954), the *ACMAF*, or *Association des Classes Moyennes Africaines*. This association stood for the protection of its members' economic interests and shortly afterwards began talks with the government authorities, to whom it proposed a series of constructive measures intended to promote the development of the middle classes and the growing prosperity of the native economy.

Similar groups were created later in other parts of the country, very often with the assistance of European settlers' associations. In 1955 the *UNICOLAF* (*Union des Colons Autochthones et Africains de la Province Orientale*) was created at Stanleyville with the assistance of the *Union des Colons de la Province Orientale*; in 1956 the *UKAT* was formed in Katanga, a section of the *ACMAF* in Kasai, the *ACMAPE* in Equator Province and the *CLAMOKI* in Kivu. The European settlers' groups which helped to found these associations lent a hand in their development and arranged to hold simultaneous congresses.

At the beginning of 1956 a census showed that there were 7,000 self-employed Africans in Leopoldville. If their families were included, they numbered in all some 30,000, or ten per cent of the total population of the Congo capital. For the territory as a whole, the figure for self-employed persons was 17,781, of whom 1,141 were professional people, 10,523 independent or semi-independent tradesmen and 6,117 craftsmen working on their own account.[1] In Leopoldville some of them earned over £7,000 a year and many had a sizeable income estimated at about £3,000 a year by the tax collectors.

Knowing how important the development of a strong middle class was to the maintenance of a political and social balance in the new Congo, the Minister of Colonies gave the leaders of the middle-class associations the opportunity to make study-trips to Belgium or to join in seminars to discuss problems in which they were interested.

Another important condition for the promotion of the African middle classes was that they should be allowed credit; the Minister therefore decided to amend the statutes of the *Société de Crédit au Colonat et à l'Industrie*, so that the African middle classes could share in its benefits. Twenty-seven loans for a total amount of about £42,000 were granted to Africans in 1956.

These decisions culminated in the creation of administrative agencies for the African middle classes within the framework of the Commercial Department of the Colonial Office and at Central and Provincial Government level, in order to co-ordinate all the problems of the African middle classes, to help them in their relations with the various administrative departments, to provide credit facilities and to organise training courses. The first of these training courses was organised from 11 to 16 February 1957 at Leopoldville by the Central Government.

In 1957, too, the *Association des Classes Moyennes Africaines* in Leopoldville set up a centre of economic and social studies to investigate the problems of its members and give them advice about their trades and crafts. Another agency

[1] Georges Brausch, 'The Problem of *Elites* in the Belgian Congo', *International Social Science Bulletin*, vol. viii, no. 3, 1956, pp. 454–7.

was set up in Brussels to enter into business relations with Belgian and European firms, to give information about export facilities and to co-ordinate with ministerial departments in Brussels.

The importance Minister Buisseret gave to the carrying out of this programme for the African middle classes proceeded from his conviction that the building up of an *élite* of independent, responsible and stable self-employed persons was an indispensable preliminary to the granting of political responsibility in the future.

Housing

It was this same concern to create a class of stable citizens which caused the Belgian administration to encourage Africans to become the owners of durably-built houses and to oblige employers to house their labour decently. These achievements in housing are the most spectacular signs of the degree of wealth of the population and particularly impress foreign visitors.

There are very few slums in the country. The lay-out of most of the urban centres has a strong traditional character, as Miss Julia Henderson, Director of the United Nations Social Affairs Department, pointed out in 1956. As the head of each family builds his own house, he can put in it everything he fancies, and thus he can organise his daily life as he wishes, which means as much as possible according to the old way of life in the rural village. These Congolese townships are picturesque, noisy and turbulent in the typical African way; there is no luxury, but neither is there poverty, and the inhabitants—feeling at home—were always happy, until political unrest started to manifest itself.

Besides these more traditional urban areas, the Belgian Government, the *Office des Cités Africaines*, the employers and the Africans themselves by their own individual efforts, joined forces to create townships that were more Western in character, with a full provision of community buildings —municipal hall, courthouse, police station, schools, dispensaries, sometimes even a hospital and a maternity ward, as in the Ruashi municipality of Elisabethville, social centres, churches, meeting halls, full water and electricity supplies, a complete road system: in short the whole infrastructure that one might expect in any up-to-date settlement.

There are no complete figures for these efforts, but those which follow may give some idea of what was done. Between 1952 and 1958 the *Office des Cités Africaines* completed more than 32,000 dwellings in the five most important towns; between 1948 and 1957 a group of eight companies carried out a project of 30,000 dwellings, representing an investment of nearly £14 million, and the Government's Loan Fund advanced about £15 million in ten years, which helped the Africans to build about fifty thousand houses. These figures do not include houses built by the Government for its own African officials and employees— probably nearly 20,000 dwellings—nor by the private initiative of hundreds of small employers, as well as the personal efforts of Africans who did not wish to apply for loans.

Besides the favourable economic conditions, expressed in an annual income which was relatively high for Africa, in the appearance of a prosperous African middle class and in the lay-out of attractive towns, another remarkable feature of Belgian colonial rule was an increase in social welfare. Economic prosperity permitted the Government and business concerns to allot considerable amounts to the financing of an elaborate system of social institutions, comprising not only the housing schemes mentioned in the previous section, but also medical care, social assistance, education and protection of labour.

Medical Services

Medical services had been established and gradually developed in the Congo from the beginning of Belgian colonisation. For a long time the principal concern of the Belgian medical officers was the eradication of sleeping sickness, but by about 1938 some five million people were being tested each year for this illness.

After World War II, a favourable budgetary situation allowed for the development of a tight network of medical services throughout the whole country to the great admiration of foreign visitors during the last years. These achievements greatly benefited the rural areas.

Under the Van Hoof-Duren project each of the 135 *territoires* (the *territoire* is an administrative subdivision with a population varying from 50,000 to 150,000 inhabitants) was provided with a rural medico-surgical centre, a surgical section, a maternity ward and a pre-natal and infant welfare advice centre.

In addition at least four principal dispensaries and several centres for secondary treatment were scattered over each *territoire*. Each medico-surgical centre was served by two doctors, one of whom was responsible for visiting the dispensaries. This project was largely achieved within the framework of the Ten Year Plan.

Alongside these government services there were many medical centres managed by private, para-state and university foundations, by the missions and by industrial and agricultural concerns.

In 1958 the Congo had the best-developed medical infrastructure in Africa, with 3,041 hospitals furnished with 86,599 beds, representing an average of 64 hospital beds for 10,000 inhabitants; the medical staff consisted of 5,663 Africans and 2,722 non-Africans, including 703 doctors, or an average of 5·2 doctors for 100,000 inhabitants; a total of 525,200 persons received hospital treatment during the year.[1]

The fact that 35 per cent of the active population of the Congo were wage-earners contributed to the diffusion of medical care, because employers are bound by law to provide free medical attention for their workers and their

[1] European Common Market, *Rapport sur la situation sociale dans les pays d'outre-mer associés à la Communauté Economique Européenne* (Brussels, 1960), pp. 132–40.

families. In that way a real system of mass medicine has been developed in the Belgian territories in Africa.

Social Assistance

Social assistance was less developed than medical assistance; for a long time it was limited to urban areas and was only available for women, because historically the first social centres which appeared in Leopoldville, Elisabethville and Coquilhatville in the years 1932, 1934, and 1938, were intended to help the wives of the wage-earners to adapt themselves to urban life. Their organisation was very empirical. We should not be too critical of the first welfare workers who were sent out to the Congo, because they were pioneers. In their search for new methods, although they knew that it was useless to transplant blindly those which had proved their worth in Europe, they were forced to take metropolitan practices as a starting-point. These were at that time the only reliable guide, and had gradually to be adapted to the new and different working conditions.

The first plans for a more rational organisation, and better adaptation to the conditions of life prevailing in Africa, came from a liberal Minister of Colonies, M. Robert Godding, who proposed a concrete scheme in a speech to the School of Social Work of Antwerp in November 1945. His plan was partly carried out by his successors. By April 1954 the number of social centres had increased to thirty-six, but they all catered only for women and used individual rather than group methods.

The rural social centres themselves, set up in 1952, were modelled on the urban social services, with groups for knitting and dressmaking, groups for expectant and young mothers, courses in domestic economy and family management, advice bureaux, home visiting, day nurseries for children, and so on. The staff worked most loyally and excellent results were achieved in individual cases. But these methods proved unsuitable for bringing about the full adjustment of African communities to present-day living conditions.

Admittedly, African urban society at that time was not highly differentiated, and little was known about its social structure. Spontaneous groupings, such as certain men's tribal associations or women's associations, tended to be regarded as survivals of a primitive social structure, ill-suited to serve as a basis for up-to-date welfare work.[1]

Meanwhile great changes had occurred elsewhere in the world in social welfare methods and the Congolese social centres were forced to adapt themselves. This task was to be fulfilled by another liberal Minister of Colonies, M. Auguste Buisseret. Social work was also extended to men. *Centres éducatifs et sociaux* were formed for them, alongside the *foyers sociaux* for women. Directions were given for a change in methods of approach: more up-to-date methods of fundamental education were to be used and those attending the centres were to take more part in organising their activities. Three schools were founded in 1956 for the training of social workers, two in Leopoldville and one in Elisabethville; the latter numbered one hundred students in January 1960. When Minister Buisseret left the Ministry there were nearly 60 social centres, 50 of them in urban areas.

Education

The Congo has for many years been ahead of the other African territories as regards education. In 1946 the published figures were very high for that time: 897,969 pupils, i.e. a rate of school attendance of 56·1 per cent, while the former French territories now associated with the Common Market numbered together only 480,870, with a school attendance rate of 11·6. In 1953 these figures were respectively 1,065,688 and 59·1 for the Congo, and 906,483 and 22·5 for the ex-French territories; in 1958–9 1,534,366 and 77·5 for the Congo and 1,667,849 and 34·8 for the former French territories. Although the latter have gradually made up some of their leeway, the Congo still remains far ahead.

[1] Georges Brausch, 'The Solvay Institute of Sociology in Belgian Africa', *International Social Science Journal*, vol. xi, no. 2, 1959, pp. 238–9.

Although the Congo has the highest developed educational system in tropical Africa, the Belgians concentrated all their efforts on a general primary education, and lagged behind in secondary, vocational and higher education, as is shown in the following comparative table:

Year	Countries	*Number of Pupils*		
		Secondary Schools	Vocational Schools	Higher Education
1946	Ex-French Territories	9,816	5,982	—
	Belgian Congo	7,540	2,079	—
1953	Ex-French Territories	35,894	16,224	69
	Belgian Congo	25,926	7,562	—
1959	Ex-French Territories	62,757	20,041	1,604
	Belgian Congo	46,370	18,194	423

This educational system was strongly influenced by the Christian missions; for a long time the latter saw schools as institutions for the recruitment of converts to their respective beliefs and consequently they had no interest in extending the school system beyond primary education. In 1958 about 94 per cent of the school population (1,446,900 pupils) were at the primary level, and within this category 97 per cent (1,406,000 pupils) were at mission schools, although a system of public schools had been created three years before. This is the highest percentage in the whole of Africa; in the same year other African territories showed the following figures: British West Africa, 90 per cent, British East Africa, 85 per cent, Cameroons, 71 per cent, Togoland 48 per cent, French Equatorial Africa 46 per cent, French West Africa 28·8 per cent.[1]

[1] 'L'Eglise en état de service', *Vivante Afrique*, no. 213, March–April, 1961.

That the missions took less interest in the other types of school is confirmed by the fact that they left more of the initiative in that field to the official education system, as is seen by the figures for 1958–9:

Type of Education	Number of Pupils			
	Official System		Private System	
Primary	40,900	3%	1,406,000	97%
Secondary	6,830	14%	39,540	86%
Technical	7,597	42%	10,597	58%
Higher	190	45%	233	55%

Mention must be made of the great strides made in education while Minister Buisseret was in charge of the Colonial Office. The following table shows that during the five-year period from 1953 to 1958 all types of education advanced further than in the *seven* previous years:

Period	Number of Years	Increase in Number of Pupils[1]		
		Primary	Secondary	Technical
1946–1953	7	143,850	18,386	5,483
1953–1958	5	414,700	20,444	10,632

The bulk of this increase benefited the mission schools and we observe too that the increase in the number of children registered at the subsidised primary schools run by the missions (445,300) was even higher than the above-mentioned figure, because the system of subsidies was extended to a large number of schools which did not previously profit by them. This is confirmed by the amounts which were paid as subsidies to the mission schools during

[1] The figures in this table, and in the others in this section, have been borrowed from the above-mentioned '*Rapport sur la situation sociale dans les pays d'outre-mer associés à la Communauté Economique Européenne*', tables 22–3, pp. 218–27.

the period 1954 to 1958. The statements of M. Buisseret's political opponents that he brought 'crippling cuts in the subsidies granted to Catholic schools' are thus refuted.[1]

Protection of African Labour

Medical care, social assistance and education are note-worthy social achievements of the Belgian colonial system in Africa, but the most remarkable of all is undoubtedly its social security system.

Social security appeared in the Congo with the great industries, and was to some extent indivisible from them because from the start the directors of these companies knew that high productivity depends on the material and social well-being of the workers. So they did not wait for legal decisions to provide housing, food, medical care, social assistance and other amenities for their workers. For years the best housing schemes, the best equipped hospitals and maternity wards, the most efficiently-run schools were to be found in the workers' settlements of the great mining companies. Before they were made obligatory by law, family allowances, compensation for illness or accidents, as well as old age pensions, were paid by these companies to their employees without any contribution from the state.

This paternalistic policy, which so irritates the champ-ions of social freedom, produced nevertheless a remarkable stabilisation of labour and encouraged the establishment of workers' settlements with a fairly good demographic equilibrium, as is shown in the following table of the labour situation at the *Union Minière du Haut Katanga*, the powerful copper mining company:

	1925	1927	1935	1939	1946	1954
Number of Workers	13,800	15,500	8,800	11,700	16,400	20,213
Number of Women per Thousand Workers	180	290	476	570	720	819
Number of Children per Thousand Workers	60	120	360	590	1,050	1,828
Annual Mortality per Thousand Workers	51	45	6·4	5	4·3	4·23

[1] Ruth Slade, *The Belgian Congo: Some Recent Changes* (London, Oxford University Press for the Institute of Race Relations, 1960), p. 40.

The Government did not stand apart from this policy, but in fact supported it with complementary measures. Minister Franck, who initiated the rapid economic expansion after the Great War, realised that tremendous human problems were involved and that steps must be taken to protect the inexperienced African workers against the dramatic consequences of the enormous changes in their traditional society under the impact of industrialisation.

His first move was of a legal kind—the elaboration of the Decree of 16 March 1922 on the labour contract, which was completed by executive ordinances of the Governor-General and the provincial governors for the protection of the health and the security of the workers. Provision of housing, food and other amenities, for instance blankets, became in many cases compulsory for employers and severe regulations were imposed on the recruitment of migrant labour, including the obligation for every employer to pay for the journey from home to the company's site, not only of the worker, but also of his whole family, as well as a return ticket for everybody when the contract was fulfilled.

Minister Franck's successor continued this policy of labour protection by the creation in December 1924 of a commission for the study of the labour problems, which recommended that future development should be carried out according to regional plans, taking into consideration the economic possibilities of an area and the availability of manpower. Labour recruitment should be allowed in a given area only if there was an excess of manpower over potential employment. So forty years ago Belgian leaders were already thinking in terms of regional planning.

In recent years, various social benefits, such as family allowances, illness and accident insurances, old age pensions, which the big companies[1] had granted voluntarily to

[1] These advantages were already fairly widespread because of the strong concentration of labour; indeed 54 per cent of African wage-earners were employed by only 190 firms each with more than 500 workers.

their workers, were extended to everyone and became compulsory; appropriate agencies were created for their administration. At the same time a certain depaternalisation of the system began; for instance the employees had to pay half of the amount of the contribution for their old age pensions; the Decree of 6 June 1956 instituted the first legal system of old age pensions for native employees in private enterprise to be enforced in an African territory South of the Sahara.

Labour Organisation

The extent to which the Belgian administration gave priority to social emancipation, before giving any thought to political emancipation, is shown by the fact that as early as 1946—that is ten years before the first political parties appeared—a system was created to prepare the Africans for the future exercise of democratic responsibilities in industrial relations. This was done through consultative councils, facilitating contact both between employers and their African personnel and between administration and workers.

This organisation, which was again the work of a liberal Minister, M. Robert Godding, included at the lowest level works councils and trade unions, then local boards of workers, and at the top regional and provincial committees of labour and social progress.

The works councils were composed of delegates from the African workers in the firm and the employer or his representative; the local committees of native workers comprised delegates from the works councils and the trade unions of a given *territoire* meeting under the chairmanship of the *administrateur de territoire*; the regional committee of labour and social progress was a tripartite board presided over by the district commissioner and composed of delegates from the administration, the employers and the workers; the provincial committee was constituted in the same way, but its chairman was the provincial commissioner (the provincial governor's deputy). All the levels of this structure could express their views and suggest measures for the improvement of labour conditions.

Excellent work was done by the regional and provincial committees, while the results obtained by the boards at the lower level varied considerably according to the personality of the territorial administrator or the employer. The facts however that no great changes were made in the system after its creation in 1946 and that the present rulers of the Congo Republic maintain it, show that it gives satisfaction and there can be no better praise than that for the Minister who was its founder.

The same legislation also provided for the creation of trade unions, but their development was very slow, as is shown in the following table, compiled from figures given in the annual reports on the administration of the Belgian Congo presented to the Legislative Councils:

Year	Number of Trade Unions	Number of Members
1950	49	5,175
1951	45	6,092
1952	59	7,067
1953—figures not available		
1954	60	7,538
1955	61	6,160
1956	69	8,829

It has been said that the Belgian administration was responsible for this situation, because it impeded the operation of the trade unions. Without any doubt the administration and the employers felt little sympathy for them; but on the other hand the trade unions did not arouse great enthusiasm among the Congolese, because they ran contrary to their traditional 'Bantu' paternalism, which conceived the relation between employer and wage-earner symbolically as that of father to son. This meant that in their view all conflicts between the parties should be settled preferably by a procedure of direct conciliation, which is possible at the level of the works council but not in the trade unions—the classic tool of class war.

Human Relations

We have mentioned in this chapter some of the tremendous changes in African society which were caused by the impact on it of Western civilisation, and expecially by accelerated industrialisation.

These influences were particularly important during World War II and immediately afterwards. Apart from benefiting the Congolese economy, the war profoundly changed the ways of life and habits of the people, although they were not directly affected by its events. The Congolese barely understood that the effort required of him, in the name of a cause which was beyond his comprehension, gave him an important role in the world; he did not know that he was being used for something which went far beyond the limits of his tribe and his area.

On the other hand the economic boom attracted to the towns the most adventurous youngsters, who wanted to free themselves from the authority of their traditional chiefs; separated from their kinsmen, exempted from sharing their wages with them, and learning new ways of life, they developed a kind of individualism which kept in check traditional solidarity. In Leopoldville for example, the African population rose from 175,000 in 1939, to 268,000 in 1954 and 350,000 in 1960.

Economic expansion, urban development, social progress, the rise in the level of education, the growth of individualism, all these factors contributed to the formation of a new Congo, in which the Africans suddenly found themselves in the presence of Europeans, no longer as the representatives of two different civilisations, but as individuals face to face with other individuals, spurred on by identical interests and preoccupations.

While in the past relations between Africans and Europeans had been relations between alien groups—each with its own hierarchy—with no desire to mix, in the new society such relations, because of the breaking of ties in each of the parent cultures, became relations between individuals of different colour.

At that stage the problem of race relations appeared and the necessity to abolish all barriers which handicap the achievement of free and direct intercourse between the members of different racial, ethnical, cultural or religious groups. This will be dealt with in the next chapter.

II. RACE RELATIONS[1]

The Colour Bar in a Plural Society

THE term 'colour bar' may be defined as unequal treatment of persons, either by the bestowal of favours or the imposition of burdens according to the colour of their skin.[2] This type of social discrimination, which is to be found in varying degrees wherever different races live side by side, prevents the weaker races from achieving a fuller life, cuts them off from all possibilities of rising and makes both races permanently conscious of their differences.[3]

A colour bar may either be enforced by law, as in the Union of South Africa and in certain Southern States of the United States of America, or just be a recognised part of conventional social life, but in that case it may be as much a class barrier as one founded purely on skin pigmentation.[4]

The colour bar which existed in the Belgian territories in Africa belonged rather to the second type and was a matter of convention. Most Belgians have never held any rigid colour prejudices, and if they do appear they cannot be said to result from any officially expressed opinions on the innate inferiority of coloured peoples. Indeed, the Belgian Government, like the British, has always, on paper, and in official statements, shown its desire to prevent explicit mention of colour bars in legal and statutory documents.

[1] This chapter is mainly based upon a lecture, 'The Abolition of the Colour Bar in the Congo', given at Study Conference No. 5 of the United Northern Rhodesia Association on 6 and 7 February 1960 at Lusaka.

[2] Frank H. Hankins, 'Social Discrimination', *Encyclopaedia of the Social Sciences*, vol. 14, p. 131.

[3] Hans Kohn, 'Race Conflict', *Encyclopaedia of the Social Sciences*, vol. 13, p. 39.

[4] Eric John Dingwall, *Race Pride and Prejudice* (London, Watts and Company, 1946), p. 163.

Intermarriage and social intercourse were never pro-
hibited legally or tacitly; children of mixed parentage
received a legal status as Europeans if they were legally
recognised by a father who was himself of European status.
No laws ever excluded Africans from employment as
skilled workers, or created a statutory barrier against the
economic advance of the most intelligent and enlightened
of them. We all know that when a train crossed the international boundary between Northern Rhodesia and the
Congo, the white engine-driver and mechanic handed the
train over to their black counterparts. Trade unions in the
Congo never tried to reserve certain jobs exclusively for
Europeans or exclude African workers from them. If most
of the higher-paid positions and the very highly skilled
occupations with which social prestige is connected were
in European hands, this was primarily because of differences in education.

Nor has the contact between the races in the Congo led
to the concentration of the best land in the hands of the
whites at the expense of the Africans. The latter had indeed
enough good land to make a living and to develop their
economy. In fact little land (2·14 per cent of the total area
of the territory) has been alienated to Europeans, and that
only in Katanga (3·29 per cent) and Kivu (2·45 per cent),
which were regarded as settlers' areas.

If certain discriminatory laws were enacted, this was not
to bar the Africans from attaining equal opportunities in
the political, social and economic fields, but primarily
because they were thought necessary to preserve existing
African institutions and to take account of African wishes.[1]

As the Africans wanted to be ruled by their own
authorities and to be judged by their own customary laws,
the Belgian administration had to organise a dual system
of administration and of justice. As the Africans had to be
protected against certain dangers, the Government passed

[1] Georges Brausch, 'Pluralisme ethnique et culturel au Congo Belge',
*Report of the XXXth Meeting of the International Institute of Differing
Civilisations*, held in Lisbon on 15 to 18 April 1957, p. 243.

certain Acts which applied only to them—regulations concerning alcoholic drinks, weapons, labour, land, etc. Other regulations were applied only to Africans to facilitate administration.

As early as 1954 and 1955 frequent statements were made by M. Buisseret, the liberal Minister of Colonies, who announced his desire to abolish gradually all discriminatory regulations in the existing laws. Some progress in this regard was made during the years when he presided over the Belgian Colonial Office, but he had to proceed slowly because of very strong hostility in conservative circles in Belgium. Therefore most of the changes were brought about only after the riots of Leopoldville in the beginning of January 1959. In the seven months between January and August 1959, forty Acts and Ordinances containing discriminatory regulations were abolished or changed.

The scope of this chapter is limited to three important subheadings—the effects of integration on the trade of hotels, cafés and places of public entertainment; integration in schools, the Civil Service and industry; the effects of new political parties on social integration.

Separate Housing.—Before discussing the first of these, it seems necessary to give some information about the former housing administration Acts in order to explain the nature of the effects of integration on the trade of hotels, cafés and places of public entertainment.

Till February 1959[1] the Congo's legislation contained fairly rigid regulations in the matter of segregation in housing, at any rate in urban areas. This segregation was enforced by a series of Acts; the first of these, dated 14 September 1898, made it compulsory to set aside land for separate areas for people of European and of coloured status when plans were established for centres of population. This measure was confirmed by the Native Settlements Ordinance of 12 February 1913, which required

---

[1] Ordinance No. 11/86 of 14 February 1959, *Administrative Bulletin*, 1959, no. 9, p. 531.

coloured workmen, servants and employees living in an
urban area to reside in special areas to be set aside by the
territorial administrator.

An Ordinance of 29 May 1926 contained provisions for
the compulsory residence of persons of European race in
separate locations in urban areas and required moreover
that persons of non-European race must obtain a permit
from the territorial administrator to be allowed to live in
the areas reserved for the European population. In certain
towns these permits were granted in large numbers to
servants, so that in Elisabethville for instance the African
population nearly outnumbered the European. But all the
Africans lived in special houses for domestic servants.

At about the same time a tendency appeared to introduce
segregation among the Africans themselves inside the
native settlements. Legislation indeed allowed the Governor-General or the provincial governors to allocate separate
areas to the inhabitants according to their personal status,
their tribal origin, their economic situation or their trade.
Fortunately these regulations were never applied.

It may seem paradoxical that very few complaints were
made by the Africans against this legislation. Many seemed
to accept the basic segregation, but they complained of the
discriminatory measures which characterised the organisation of each of these areas. Thus they asked for the abolition of the curfew and for freedom of movement at night,
similar to that enjoyed by the Europeans in their areas.[1]

An Ordinance of 14 February 1959 abolished all these
discriminatory regulations. In implementation of this Act
the government services and some private companies made
it possible for those of their African staff in employment
similar to that of their European staff to be housed in the
European residential area. Most of the Africans preferred
however to stay in the African areas. The first of them who
chose to live in the European residential areas had no
complaints about incidents based on race prejudice.

[1] Brausch, 'Pluralisme ethnique et culturel au Congo Belge', p. 253.

But because the very great majority of the African population and the entire African *élite* lived separately from the Europeans, the social life of the Africans was concentrated in their own neighbourhoods and for the most part they went to European hotels, cafés, restaurants or places of public entertainment only if they wished to meet European friends or were invited by them. The converse was true with regard to visits by Europeans to the African neighbourhoods.

Hotels, Cafés and Restaurants.—In fact, Congolese law never forbade the accommodation of Africans in European hotels, but the question seldom arose until African leaders began to travel, i.e. not before the years 1949–50. The first Africans who asked for accommodation in European hotels were visitors from other African territories; the problem was solved by giving them facilities in the luxury guest-houses which the Sabena Airline had set up at its air terminals.

When the Africans of the Congo became members of the different government and provincial councils, committees and commissions, the need arose to give them accommodation, and as the official services did not wish to be accused of practising discrimination, they booked rooms for preference in first-class hotels. Because of this tendency one would usually find Africans in the best hotels and not in the modest ones, which were patronised primarily by the European middle classes. No noteworthy incidents were caused by this integration of the African *élite* in the hotels, and no case was ever reported of the boycotting of such hotels by Europeans because of colour prejudice. Experience showed that an hotel which kept up its standards, notwithstanding the admission of an African clientele, would suffer no ill effects.

Again no segregation law ever determined that cafés or restaurants should be reserved for only one racial group. Africans have always been allowed to consume non-alcoholic drinks in cafés or to have meals in restaurants frequented by Europeans but they did not do so until about 1946. Even then they went to such establishments only if they were invited as guests by Europeans.

One factor which kept Africans away from European cafés and restaurants was that the law did not allow the owners to serve alcoholic drinks to them. This gave them the feeling that they were not allowed in these establishments at all, especially since certain café and restaurant proprietors, on their own initiative, refused them admission and no law existed to protect Africans against such discrimination.

A change was brought about in this matter by an Ordinance of 1 July 1955; according to this, café and restaurant owners were allowed to serve beer, wine and all other alcoholic drinks to certain categories of Africans belonging to the *élite*, namely those who possessed a 'carte du mérite civique' or had obtained their 'immatriculation'[1]. The Governor-General gave wide publicity to this Act and gave special instructions to provincial governors and the chairmen of Chambers of Commerce for its immediate and general application.

This publicity caused a mass movement toward white cafés, and this was accompanied by various excesses, such as noisy demonstrations, with Africans behaving like *nouveaux riches*, drinking toasts in champagne at pavement cafés where Europeans were modestly drinking their glasses of beer. A certain nervousness was observed among the Europeans and sometimes even a tendency to boycott these cafés.

---

[1] Wishing to ensure for Africans a gradual development towards European juridical status, the Government created in 1948 the 'carte du mérite civique' which assured its holder of a certain assimilation in matters of court procedure, movement at night and some other advantages. The 'immatriculation' was a registration in the category of civilised persons granted to an African by a court ruling, preceded by an enquiry proving that the applicant was living according to European standards. An 'immatriculé' was allowed to become subject to the system of Congolese civil law and to be assimilated to Europeans in matters of juridical organisation, procedure and competence, movement at night and other matters.

The introduction of the new system was, however, responsible for only a few incidents, such as one caused by a foreigner who was convicted for inciting racial hatred and expelled from the country. This example seems to have been salutary to other white people who did not completely agree with the new liberal regulations. If in the beginning some European customers protested, made rude observations or only glanced in a shocked or astonished way at the Africans, most of them very quickly became accustomed to meeting Africans in white cafés or restaurants.

But the Africans soon realised that the drinks in these white cafés were far more expensive than in the bars in their own neighbourhood and that the atmosphere was less cheerful—hence when the attraction of novelty wore off their patronage decreased and became normal. At the end of 1959 Africans freely entered all cafés and restaurants situated in the European areas; but those who were encountered in these places were usually chiefs, delegates to official meetings, or the guests of Europeans.

Shops.—Generally speaking, shops have always been open to all races, but some shopkeepers were on their own initiative guilty of discriminatory practices such as the provision of separate entries, counters and payment-windows for each racial group.

After 1954 the Government authorities and the Chambers of Commerce made several appeals to traders to do away with these practices. As many of them did not respond to these appeals the Government issued an Ordinance on 1 October 1959 providing for heavy fines and, in case of repeated offences, the closing of the establishment for a maximum of two months. The fear of these severe sanctions had an immediate effect and segregation in shops had disappeared everywhere by the beginning of 1960.

Places of Public Entertainment.—No real colour bar has ever been applied between Africans and Europeans in places of public entertainment such as theatres, cinemas,

LIBRARY
College of St. Francis
JOLIET, ILL.
33605

circuses or sports events. If at such events a separation was observed between the two racial groups, this was because of the great differences in the prices of tickets.

Thus for instance there was generally a great difference in the entrance prices at sports events and circuses, varying from the best-placed seats to standing-room. As a rule Europeans paid for seats and Africans only for standing-room, although more and more Africans of the *élite* paid the higher prices to establish their prestige among their own people.

For a long time no Africans went to the theatre because they took little interest in this art. It was only in about 1946 that dramatic arts started to develop among them, along with the inclination to patronise the European theatre, but again the higher prices, generally from a hundred to a hundred and fifty francs (from fourteen shillings to a guinea), were a real economic bar cutting them off from such entertainment.

At the cinema the situation was more complicated, since an Ordinance of the Governor-General provided that all films to be shown to Africans had to be censored by a special commission. Since the film distributors systematically neglected to submit their films to these commissions of censorship, the European cinemas were not allowed to admit Africans. An Ordinance of 21 September 1959 set up a general commission of censorship for films and there was no longer any differentiation between the censorship of films for Europeans and for Africans. After that Africans had access to the European cinemas. In Elisabethville, however, there were rarely more than fifteen Africans in the audience at each meeting, most of them university students. Here again the high prices of the seats (fifty francs or seven shillings) prevented Africans from going to the cinema more often.

Schools.—The differences between the two races in ways of life, in thought and in speech obliged the governing powers to create a dual system of education. African and

European children went to segregated schools until 1948.

The first move towards racial desegregation in education was made when legally recognised or adopted Euro-african children were admitted to schools which had until then been reserved for European children. In 1950 admission was extended to non-recognised Euro-african children as well as to African children who were living in a family environment similar to that of a European family. The admission of these African children was decided by a provincial school commission after an enquiry into the moral, cultural and intellectual standards of the parents, and their financial means, which had to be sufficient to allow the child to finish his secondary studies.

In 1953, 21 African children were admitted to European schools throughout the Congo, in 1954, 75, in 1956, 203, in 1957, 446, in 1958, 850 and in 1959, 1,493 (see Table I).

In about 1956-7 the names of the schools were changed from 'European' and 'Native' to 'de régime métropolitain' and 'de régime congolais'; at the beginning of 1959 this terminology was again changed to 'écoles de programme métropolitain' and 'de programme congolais'. In 1959, all the special regulations with regard to the admission of African children to metropolitan schools were abolished and they were now subject to exactly the same conditions as European children.

The most recent statistics for African pupils in metropolitan schools in the whole Congo just before Independence are not available, but those for the schools in Elisabethville may give an idea of the progress of school integration up to that time. During the school year 1956–7 the three metropolitan schools of Elisabethville had only 70 non-European pupils (Asians, Africans and Euro-africans) in a total enrolment of 3,625, i.e. not even 2 per cent. At the beginning of 1960 there were 435 African pupils in a total enrolment of 4,011, i.e. nearly 11 per cent. This percentage was of course higher in the lower grades, namely 13·8 per cent in the three primary schools, and in one of them—that of the *Athénée Royal* (a state-administered high school) it reached 25·7 per cent. In the first grade of this latter establishment, 42·6 per cent. of the pupils were Africans. More and more schools, especially the secondary schools but also the primary ones in the urban areas, adopted the Belgian metropolitan programme.

Another step towards the establishment of scholastic equality between Africans and Europeans was the inauguration in 1954 of state-administered education for Africans, parallel to the systems of education administered by religious organisations, either on behalf of the state or with state subsidies, which had existed in the Congo since the beginning of Belgian colonisation. This measure gave Africans a choice of schools in line with their personal convictions, a choice which had been open to Europeans since 1946.

While the metropolitan schools were opening their doors ever wider to African children, a new step towards better racial integration was taken in 1955 with the creation of new inter-racial *Athénées* and the opening of Lovanium University at Kimuenza, followed in 1956 by the opening of the official University of the Belgian Congo and Ruanda-Urundi at Elisabethville.

By 1960 all the schools were officially inter-racial and European children could even be admitted into schools of the Congolese programme. However it was expected then that the former Native schools would for a long time to come be inter-racial only in name, although in certain localities European children did go to them because there was no metropolitan school nearby. Nevertheless these developments showed the intention of the Belgian administration to abolish all racial discrimination in education by encouraging racial integration in both European and Native schools.

Nevertheless, some voices expressed the fear that a completely desegregated education would tend to promote only European cultural values and would neglect those of the African civilisation. Others also pointed out that valuable teaching systems existed in traditional Africa, which were adapted to the African mentality, and that it would be a mistake to ignore them. These people maintained that it might even be useful to test their validity in a pilot training school for teachers.

Civil Service.—Among the discriminatory measures that were most difficult to get away from were those which existed in the Civil Service. Until 1959 there were two separate branches: one for auxiliary staff members, who had not completed their secondary studies and were employed in the lower grades, and another for the higher staff, recruited only from among those with either a diploma of completed metropolitan secondary studies or a university degree.

The auxiliary posts were reserved for Africans; no European was admitted to them. A European who had not completed his secondary studies could only be employed in the government service on a temporary contract.

On the other hand, admission to the higher grades was reserved for persons of Belgian or Luxembourg nationality. Since Africans were not legally regarded as Belgian nationals, but rather as Belgian subjects, they did not qualify for admission to those positions.

As long as opportunities for secondary and university education were limited, there was no need to change the law in this regard. But from 1953 onwards it was admitted that certain African officials in the auxiliary grades had acquired professional qualifications, which entitled them to accede to the lowest level of the higher grades.

There were two opposing points of view about this. The jurists proposed that plans for a new unified service, to include officials of all ranks, should be drawn up by the administration and discussed by a joint commission composed of government delegates, European civil servants and African auxiliaries. This would however be a long-term procedure.

On the other hand, more practical-minded persons were of the opinion that if an African was proved to have the necessary qualifications, he should immediately be commissioned at the lowest level of the higher grades. Meanwhile the jurists would have time to draw up the new system.

The administration adopted the first viewpoint, and this resulted in dissatisfaction among the African auxiliaries, as well as among European civil servants.

While the number of African auxiliaries qualified to claim appointments as civil servants was only two or three in 1953, it grew rapidly to about 40 in 1956 and about 400 in 1958. The continual postponement of a decision in this matter created a feeling among the Africans that the administration was unwilling to admit them to the Civil Service.

Preoccupied by budgetary considerations, the administration was afraid to give the new African civil servants the same salaries as the Europeans earned and it therefore decided in 1958 to set up for the higher grades new wage scales which would be much lower than before. This news created a violent reaction among the European civil servants, which resulted in demonstrations against the Minister of Colonies, when he visited Elisabethville in February 1958.

An agreement was at last reached in March–April 1958 and the new unified system came into effect on 1 January 1959. Between this date and the end of August 742 Africans were appointed to posts which were previously reserved for Europeans. However the number remained low in the provinces of the interior, such as Katanga, where on 1 January 1960 only 33 Africans had been appointed to the higher grades—17 agricultural officers, 7 health officers, 5 clerks and 4 territorial officers.

Despite the remarkable effort which had been made, these figures remained too small for a country which was on the threshold of independence. Therefore the Government decided upon additional measures to accelerate the africanisation of the Civil Service.

In each *territoire* the administrator was asked to choose his best African auxiliary and to send him to a training centre. After one year's training and a satisfactory practical examination, these auxiliaries would have been qualified for appointments as territorial officers. In this way 150 African territorial officers might have been nominated by the beginning of 1961.

A similar accelerated training was to be given to African auxiliaries in the central and provincial government services, as for instance the Katanga provincial service, which chose 33 African auxiliaries with certificates of secondary education in the Congolese programme. After passing a series of psycho-technical tests, they were to receive one year's training under the supervision of a *chef de bureau*. They would be given a certificate of proficiency if they passed a practical examination and would be considered as qualified for appointment as clerks.

But it was not enough to admit Africans to the lowest level of the Civil Service; it was also necessary to give them responsible and supervisory jobs.

The first Congolese appointed to a higher post was M. Roger Bolamba, editor-in-chief of *La Voix du Congolais*, a monthly review published by the Government Information Service. He was later appointed, in September 1955, as an *Attaché de Cabinet* to the Minister of Colonies. Although the opposition party of the moment severely criticised this appointment, the example set in 1955 by a liberal Minister was followed in 1958 when the opposition returned to power. At the same time, at the request of the new Minister of Colonies, another African was appointed as *Attaché de Cabinet* to the Governor-General.

After the riots of January 1959 *Attachés de Cabinet* were also appointed to the staff of all the provincial governors, district commissioners and territorial administrators, to advise them on African affairs.

At the same time an African (M. Bolikango, who is at the time of writing Vice-President of the Ileo Government) was appointed to the office of Assistant General Commissioner of Information and another to be General Commissioner of Youth. Both of them were at the head of government services which were to be of capital importance to the new Congo.

Africans were also appointed by the administration to the boards of directors of business concerns in which the government had the chief financial interest, namely in Sabena airlines and in the Institute of Inga, set up to develop the power potential of the Lower Congo.

Jobs in Industry.—Integration in industry had been moving forward in the Congo for a long time. Since the beginning of industrialisation, Africans had been trained as qualified workers and no objection had ever been made to such training, for instance by European trade unions. Africans generally operated all the machinery used in industry, in the mines and in road-building. The supervisors, however, were all Europeans.

Certain supervisory jobs were entrusted to Africans, who were given the title of 'capita', in places where European supervisors were called 'contremaîtres'. At the end of 1959, eighteen Africans were in such posts at the *Union Minière du Haut Katanga*, and eight of them had been advanced to the European wage scale, while ten were just below it. Six Africans were doing highly qualified work which was ordinarily done by Europeans.

Certainly too little had been done in this direction; there were no African engineers, because until then no higher technical courses had been provided. A few African students are now working towards a university degree in engineering, but their number is very small.

Political Integration

Integration in the political field may be reached in two ways: either by the integration of Africans into European political parties, or by the integration of Europeans into African political parties.

Integration of Africans into European Political Parties.—The first political activities among Africans in the Congo were fostered by Belgian political organisations, namely by

Belgian trade unions with political orientations. The first Belgian trade union to be established in the Congo was the *Confédération des Syndicats Chrétiens du Congo*, supported by the *Parti Social Chrétien* in Belgium. Its first office was established at Leopoldville in 1946. The *Fédération Générale du Travail de Belgique*, which has a strong socialist emphasis, followed in 1951, but did not become active among the Africans before 1953. Until 1954 these trade unions were the only organisations which fostered political activity among either Europeans or Africans.

Open political activity started in the Congo in 1955 with the creation of liberal and socialist fraternal organisations, called *amicales*.

The trade unions as well as the *amicales* were presided over by Europeans. Africans were accepted as members and some of them even elected to the committees, but at that stage there were not enough African members for them to obtain a majority on the committees. This first stage in the penetration of the Congo by political doctrines was important, however, because it was in these Belgian political organisations that many of the present leaders received their political training.

M. Patrice Lumumba, leader of the *Mouvement National Congolais (M.N.C.)* and first Prime Minister of the Congo Republic, was in 1956 a member of the *Amicale Libérale* of Stanleyville; M. Cyrille Adoula, vice-president of the dissident branch of the *M.N.C.* and Minister of the Interior in the Ileo Government, was until 1959 a very active leader of the *Amicale Socialiste* of Leopoldville; M. Arthur Pinzi, one of the leaders of the *Abako* and past president of the *Association du Personnel Indigène du Congo (A.P.I.C.)*, was a member of the *Amicale Libérale* of Leopoldville, as was also M. Paul Bolya, the president of the *Parti National du Progrès (P.N.P.)* and Minister of State in the Cabinet of M. Patrice Lumumba.

Among the four African mayors elected by the municipal councils of Elisabethville in January 1958, two claimed

membership of the *Amicale Libérale* and one was a member
of the socialist trade union movement.

Up to 1958 it seemed that many of the African leaders
had been successfully integrated into Belgian political
organisations; a list of the present Congolese leaders shows
that at that time the most representative among them
were thus formally incorporated.

The following months showed, however, that this
integration was only superficial and temporary. Well
educated, intelligent and quick to understand European
political doctrines, the first African politicians observed
that these doctrines needed to be adapted to the African
mentality if mass movements were to be created from them.
Here the Belgian politicians failed: they were unable to
understand that liberalism and socialism had to be afri-
canised and re-thought according to principles of African
philosophy. In Brussels the Belgian liberals who in 1957
supported the demands of the Africans for an africanisation
of liberal principles were nicknamed 'blue Mau-Mau'
(blue being the colour of the Belgian Liberal Party) by the
higher officials of the party.

On the other hand the Belgian political parties could not
free themselves from the paternalistic attitude inherent in
most European institutions in Africa. They were persuaded
that the African *élite* on which they concentrated their
attention was not yet mature enough to go its own way.
Lacking confidence in the *élite*, they were afraid to let it
create popular political movements among Africans. Even
very progressive Belgian politicians believed that the
evolution should be slow; the most revolutionary among
them thought in terms of a thirty-year plan.[1]

But when at the beginning of 1958 the parties were in
danger of losing their popularity with their African
followers, the Belgian Liberal and Socialist Parties tried to
avoid secession by permitting the creation at Leopoldville
of a Congolese Liberal Party by M. Pinzi, president of an

[1] A. A. J. van Bilsen, 'Un plan de trente ans pour l'émancipation
politique de l'Afrique Belge', *Dossier de l'Action Sociale Catholique*, 1956.

all-African trade union, and a Socialist Action Movement of which M. Adoula was the leader. These action groups came too late to resist the approaching wave of nationalism.

Gradually these first African leaders left the Belgian political organisations which had given them their initial political training and created their own action groups. This desertion started in October 1958, with the founding of the *M.N.C.* by M. Patrice Lumumba, former member of the *Amicale Libérale*.

Integration of Europeans into African Political Parties.—The first signs of the reverse trend, the founding of specifically African political movements into which Europeans were eventually to be integrated, appeared in July 1956 in the political manifesto of *Conscience Africaine*. This statement was prepared by a group of Catholic Africans, among them M. Ileo, second Prime Minister of the Congo Republic, with the help of one or two European Catholics teaching at Lovanium University, who remained in the background. The manifesto was supposed to be a reaction—although this was not clearly stated—against those who had tried to integrate Africans into the Belgian Liberal and Socialist Parties. It called for political emancipation according to a thirty-year plan—showing Van Bilsen's influence. Although this statement was the first public expression of the Africans' desire to take the lead in their own emancipation, it remained rather vague in its proposals. The counter-manifesto published in August 1956 by the *Abako*, or *Association des Bakongo pour l'Unification, la Conservation et l'Expansion de la Langue Kikongo*, was much clearer.

This document rejected categorically the intervention of the Belgian political parties, but accepted the presence of Europeans in the future Congo on condition that they would co-operate with African programmes. *Abako* grew rapidly into a mass movement in the Lower Congo and Europeans gradually affiliated with it in the following years, sometimes from innate conviction, but mostly for reasons of fear or opportunism. At the end of 1959 one

thousand Europeans, including officials, traders, missionaries, industrialists and the directors of important businesses,
were members of *Abako*.

For some time this reverse trend of integration was
limited to the Lower Congo. It was not until October 1957
that similar African political movements grew up elsewhere.
At that time, with the help of a Belgian barrister, a group
of Catholic Africans in Elisabethville created the *Union
Congolaise*, to counter liberal and socialist propaganda in
the first communal election campaign of December 1957.

On 26 August 1958, two days after an important, frank
and generous speech by General de Gaulle at Brazzaville,
a group of Congolese leaders in Leopoldville, belonging to
various existing political movements, sent a collective
petition to the Minister of Colonies, asking for immediate
political reforms. Several of these leaders belonged to
Belgian political movements; their petition was the signal
that they intended to go their own way in the future.

This separation was accomplished in October, when most
of the leaders joined in the creation of one or another of the
many nationalist parties. Nevertheless many of them
maintained their affiliations with the Belgian political
organisations which had received them in the past. But
these links with their parent parties had only a symbolic
meaning for them.

From then on an enormous number of new political
parties were founded, most of them of a local, tribal or
regional character. Many of them amalgamated into
groups of parties, which in turn formed super-groups. It
was very difficult to get an accurate picture of the political
situation at a given moment, because the alliances were
changing continually. In the face of this situation the
European political parties definitely abandoned their idea
of trying to integrate Africans into their structure.

Did these new political parties encourage social integration? We must not forget that they were formed in
reaction against the paternalism of the European political
parties and the lack of freedom and sympathy which the

African leaders encountered in them. Thus the basic tendency of these nationalistic movements was opposition to European domination. Nevertheless most of the nationalist movements had European advisers, even the most extremist ones such as the *M.N.C.*, the *Abako* and the *Parti du Peuple*, and all admitted European members.

The more moderate parties such as the *P.N.P.* in the Kasai and the *Province Orientale* and the Conakat in Katanga based their electoral programmes on partnership and integration with the Europeans and won the municipal elections of December 1959 on this platform. In many places one or more European candidates figured in the electoral lists of these African political parties and often such a candidate was elected by the African voters.

At the end of 1959 there was a feeling that if the new political parties encouraged social integration, it was coming about in a totally different way from that generally envisaged by the Europeans. The European community was steadily becoming integrated politically with the African *élite*, instead of the Africans being integrated with the white population, as in the United States of America.

Integration and Acculturation

The integration of the European community with the African *élite* was a condition which the new political parties of the Congo wanted to impose upon the Europeans just before Independence, but they wanted this integration not to remain only political, but to become general. Thus for instance it was announced that in the future Independent Congo the Belgians would be treated as Congolese citizens if they applied for Congolese nationality. Some favoured a dual Congolese and Belgian nationality on the condition that the Africans should also benefit from this status and enjoy in Belgium the same privileges as Belgian nationals. But before the European and African communities could be completely integrated socially and culturally, the over-all problem of human relations between Africans and Europeans had to be reconsidered.

Were the Europeans psychologically prepared for such an abdication? Certainly not! Too many Europeans still regarded the phenomenon of acculturation resulting from the contact between the European and African civilisations as an evolution from an inferior stage to a higher one. They were convinced that Western culture was superior to that of the Africans and that the political, social, economic, family and trade union institutions of the white men were superior to the tribal, clan and corporate institutions of the African people.[1]

Undoubtedly certain of the African intellectual *élite* shared this view. But the great majority of Africans and a fraction—much larger than was supposed—of the intellectual *élite*, considered the problem objectively as a phenomenon of contact, a phenomenon of meeting between civilisations, their own and that of the West. According to them European superiority was established only in the technical field. They shrank in distaste from embracing European principles in the political, social and family fields and they continued to prefer many of their traditional institutions.

The Congolese people wanted to emerge from their state of under-development and asked for assistance primarily in the economic and technical fields. But they wanted this technical and economic development to be achieved, as far as possible, within the framework of their own institutions, in order to reduce to a minimum the disequilibrium and the stress which are created by the interpenetration of traditional and Western values, attitudes and motivations in the same social bodies.

Technical and economic assistance needs to be adapted to the traditional structure. Thus a new and very delicate

[1] Georges Brausch, 'Applied Anthropology in the Belgian Territories in Africa (An Experience of Integration of the Tribal Institutions into the Pattern of the New Social Action in Central Africa)', *Selected Papers of the Fifth International Congress of Anthropological and Ethnological Sciences*, Philadelphia, 1–9 September 1956 (University of Pennsylvania Press, Philadelphia, 1960) pp. 755–763.

problem appears: how to ensure the integration of the technical and economic structures of the West into the traditional structure of less-developed African communities and at the same time to interest these communities in their own development so as to obtain not only their agreement but also their active participation and the co-operation of each individual.

In the following chapter we shall show what was done by the Belgian administration to promote the participation of the Congolese in the government and development of their country.

III. CONGOLESE PARTICIPATION IN GOVERNMENT

THE Belgians first came to the Congo in 1879 under the auspices of the International Association of the Congo, which concluded treaties with a large number of African chiefs. In 1885 the Treaty of Berlin recognised this association as a sovereign power. It took the name of the Congo Free State, and the King of the Belgians became its Sovereign. In 1908 King Leopold II transferred his sovereign powers to the Belgian state and the Congo became a Belgian colony.

We must bear in mind that before the Belgians came to Central Africa, the Congo did not exist as a *political unit* (as for instance did Egypt, Ethiopia, Tunis, Morocco, Basutoland, Swaziland, Rwanda or Burundi). The Congo was a political unit when power was transferred on 30 June 1960, but this was the result of Belgian colonial rule, and it had taken seventy-five years to make one political unit out of all its territories.

This does not mean that there was no political organisation at all. On their arrival in Central Africa the Belgians found a multitude of tribes, large and small, which were the real political units of the country.

The political and administrative organisation which Belgian rule established in the Congo was a result of these two factors and it comprised a system of local government based on the traditional African political units, i.e. small kingdoms and tribes, and a Central Government created by the Belgians.

We shall examine to what extent the Congolese participated in each of these two levels of government under Belgian rule.

Local Government[1]

We have already mentioned that the first political relations established between Africans and Europeans were based upon the treaties made by the pioneers with the traditional chiefs. These treaties were very often sanctioned by the exchange of blood or other traditional rituals which accompanied the conclusion of agreements according to native custom. The chiefs were confirmed in their functions by the explorers and they were allowed to exercise them as in the past. At this stage, the native communities kept their characteristics, their social structure and their institutions untouched.

But before long European pressure became stronger and the terms of the treaties of friendship became those of treaties of overlordship, through which the traditional chiefs recognised the suzerainty of the Congo Free State. This spirit is clearly seen in the Decree of 6 October 1891, which aimed at integrating the native political institutions as units of local government into the framework of the newly-created administration of the Free State.

A difficulty occurred here. The traditional political units were very complicated pyramidal structures with hamlets and villages at the base, then groups of parent villages, then leagues or confederations of villages, then tribes, peoples and sometimes kingdoms.

The problem was to decide which level of the pyramid should be recognised by the Free State as a *chefferie*, which was the name given to these units of local government. At first the village level was adopted, in imitation of Belgian practice; but although most Congolese villages are large in area, their population does not generally exceed two to three hundred inhabitants.

It was difficult to found a sound administration on a sprinkling of small villages; therefore larger units were progressively adopted as time went on. Nevertheless the

[1] For a detailed account of the development of local government in the Congo, see Georges Brausch, 'Communes africaines', *Revue de l'Université de Bruxelles*, 9th year (January–April 1957), pp. 230–59.

chefferies recognised by the Belgian administration continued to be too small. In 1917 they numbered 6,095.

In 1920 Minister Louis Franck recommended the constitution of large administrative units provided with modern government institutions. These were to be called *secteurs* and were groups of small tribal units, too small to be administered satisfactorily by themselves. The first *secteurs* were created in 1922 in the Eastern Province, but it was eleven years before the system was made general, by the Decree of 5 December 1933.

The number of *chefferies* was reduced from 2,496 in 1935 to 1,070 in 1940, 594 in 1945, 476 in 1950 and 432 in 1955; thus in twenty years 2,064 *chefferies* disappeared. During the same period the *secteurs* in which these *chefferies* were absorbed increased in number from 57 in 1935 to 383 in 1940, 498 in 1945, 517 in 1950; by 1955 they had decreased to 509 because of a decision to create large *secteurs*. By 1955 there were 941 local government units for a total rural population of 9,712,547, giving an average population of a little more than 10,000 inhabitants to a unit, about the same average as in Belgian municipalities. In 1960 the number of units had fallen to about 900 for a total rural population of more than ten and a half million; so the average population of such a unit was about 12,000.

The adoption of a system of large units enabled a legal status to be given to most of the traditional political communities, even some of the very large ones like the Baswaga tribe of the Lubero territory (Kivu), which has a population of over 150,000. The large kingdoms which extended over several territories, such as the Lunda, the Bayaka and others, could not be included in this system and only their subdivisions were given legal status as administrative units.

Each traditional community was included in the *chefferie* or in the *secteur*, with its whole pyramidal organisation, and all its subdivisions maintained their traditional rights. Thus all administrative instructions had to pass through all the levels of the traditional hierarchy, a characteristic feature of indirect rule.

These rural units (*chefferies* and *secteurs*) are administered by chiefs, assisted by councils, which were composed until 1957 exclusively of traditional native dignitaries.

Since 1891 the *chefferies*, and later on the *secteurs*, were gradually provided with embryonic administrative departments, to prepare them for their role as modern administrative units. But the man who gave his name to the orientation of this system towards a form of municipal government was Minister Louis Franck, who can really be regarded as Belgium's Lord Lugard. He gave them their own budget, their own taxes and self-government. This evolution was completed by the Decree of 10 May 1957, which established a system of popular consultation for the constitution of the councils.

Most of these units now possess a complete administrative infrastructure, comprising a secretariat, a treasury, a court and a police force, road maintenance services, an agricultural staff, schools, one or more dispensaries, sometimes even a maternity ward, a social centre and farm settlement scheme.

But the Belgian administration also had to face the problem of organising the masses of people who had left their traditional environment to flock to the urban areas; in 1959 they numbered 3,096,269, or 22 per cent of the total population of the Congo.

Before 1957 this urban population was organised into *cités indigènes* and *centres extra-coutumiers*. The status of *cité indigène* was given to urban centres which were too small to stand by themselves administratively; each had a *chef de cité* and a council, but no administrative departments and no financial autonomy. Larger urban areas were organised into *centres extra-coutumiers*, with a structure very similar to that of the *chefferie* and the *secteur* and with the same equipment of administrative departments.

By the Decree on the *Statut des Villes* of 26 March 1957, Minister Buisseret created two new types of urban unit, the *commune* and the *ville*. The *commune* was administered by a burgomaster, assisted by a municipal council elected by universal suffrage; many of the *centres extra-coutumiers* were converted into *communes*. The *ville* was a federation of *communes* in the same urban area. Leopoldville for instance is a *ville* consisting of twelve *communes*.

This survey shows that the Belgian colonial administration strongly encouraged the building of an autonomous self-ruling system of local government (similar to the British system of native authorities), while as we shall see in the following section the establishment of an autonomous, self-ruling Central Government was persistently discouraged.

The chief reasons for this policy are, first, as we indicated before, that when the Belgians came to the Congo, they found self-ruling tribes and they recognised them as units of local government; and secondly, that the Belgians also thought that these local government units should be the foundations upon which to build up a Central Government in the future. We shall come back to this point later.

Undoubtedly this *system of local government*, together with the *economic infrastructure* and the *social achievements*, was for years the chief strength of Belgian colonial rule. Everywhere in the world the ordinary man is concerned above all with local everyday matters, and these matters can only be settled by local government authorities. A good and effective local government system is able to satisfy most of his needs especially if those needs are still inconsiderable in monetary terms, as is the case in under-developed areas. In the Congo both the rural and urban populations could thus settle all their problems within the framework of the local government units and so for a long time few of them gave any thought to the problems of central government.

The system of local government enforced by the Belgians in the Congo may well leave in the memory of the

Congolese the impressions so well expressed by N. U. Akpan in 'An Epitaph to Indirect Rule':

> Our old mother indirect rule
> Liked, disliked and misunderstood
> Thou didst play thy part well
> Laying solid foundations for days ahead
> We shall not forget thee whate'er we do.

Local government indeed paved a way to democracy in the Congo. History teaches that the appearance and the development of local government institutions usually coincide with the spread of movements of emancipation and democratisation: the Greek cities of antiquity, the charters of the free towns of the Middle Ages, the municipal constitutions of the nineteenth century all coincided with periods when democratic doctrines flourished.

Real democracy demands the fullest participation of the people in the management of the state. In a strong centralised country where the citizens merely elect a hundred or several hundred deputies, this participation remains rather symbolic. But it becomes a reality when not necessarily all the citizens, but a great number of them, meet to discuss the problems of government. This happened in the Congo when the council meetings of the *chefferies* and the *secteurs* were attended by hundreds of tribesmen or citizens, and not only the council members but any tribesman or citizen was allowed to—and in fact very often did—express an opinion on the problems of the local government unit.

Since 1952, however, certain of the Congolese, especially among the intelligentsia, complained that this system restricted the growth of an autonomous African political life. They wanted a pyramidal system in the Congo similar to the native administration structure of Rwanda-Burundi, which comprises *sous-chefferies*, *chefferies* and *pays*; Rwanda and Burundi each had the status of a *pays*.

The suggestion was made that the existing *secteurs* and *chefferies* should be grouped into new units at a higher level, something like leagues of *chefferies* or confederations of *secteurs* and *chefferies* belonging to the same ethnic grouping; this formula would have enabled the scattered parts of the former large political units, like the Lunda kingdom, the Luba empire, the Azande sultanate, the Bayaka nation and many others, to be brought together again and re-unified on a new democratic basis but with common origins and cultural similarities taken into account.[1]

The existing *chefferies* and *secteurs* would have kept their present status, but they would gave sent deputies to a Grand Council of the *pays* or the *canton*, or whatever name was given to these new administrative units. The possibility was considered of transferring to them some or even all of the powers of the territorial and district administration, and appointing the former territorial and district staff as technical assistants at the new administrative level. This would automatically have achieved the complete african-isation of the lower grades of central administration (see Table II).

This policy of grouping the existing divisions into larger units should of course have been undertaken with care and consideration for the existing situation. Such a federation should certainly not have been imposed arbitrarily; it needed to express the will of the native communities them-selves.

The 'Statut des Villes' of 26 March 1957 achieved some such grouping for the urban areas, by converting the existing *centres extra-coutumiers* into *communes* and joining *communes* in the same urban area together into *villes*. But the Belgian administration categorically refused to con-sider a similar policy for the rural areas, although it was supported by many traditional chiefs and also by many of the emerging political leaders. A few months later these demands were to find expression in the creation of a multitude of ethnical, political parties. Their influence became clearly visible at the legislative elections of May

---

[1] Georges Brausch, 'Construction d'une nation africaine', *Synthèses*, 11th year (June 1956), p. 217.

1960, when they were responsible for the very wide dispersion of votes upon a large number of electoral lists and also the distribution of seats in the two legislative assemblies among a large number of different parties.

These claims were the first manifestations of the African desire for some formula of self-government beyond local government, and the fact that they were rejected without careful study created a feeling of frustration, which was to grow as subsequent proposals were also refused. The Belgian administration did not realise that in the period from 1956 to 1958 the *chefferies*, *secteurs*, *centres extra-coutumiers* and *communes* no longer provided a sufficient outlet for the political ambitions of the younger generation.

Central Government

From 1926 onwards the central administration was organised in the Congo at four levels, those of general, provincial, district and territorial government. The central administration was situated in Leopoldville; it was headed by a Governor-General, assisted by a government council. There were at first four provinces, and six since 1934;[1] each was headed by a provincial governor, assisted by a provincial council. Each province was divided into a number of districts, administered by district commissioners; recently the total number of districts was twenty-four, which means an average population of over 500,000 per district. There were never any councils at this level. Each district was subdivided into a number of *territoires* ruled by territorial administrators; there were 135 *territoires* in recent years and since 1957 they have had their own councils.

Just as local government was the monopoly of the Congolese, central government was reserved for the Belgians. Until 1946 Africans took no part in it and even

[1] Before 1934 Lower Congo (capital Leopoldville), Equator Province (Coquilhatville), Eastern Province (Stanleyville), Katanga (Elisabethville); in 1934 an administrative reorganisation created two new provinces, Kasai (capital Luluabourg) and Kivu (Bukavu).

in the administrative departments they were until 1954 relegated to subordinate jobs, as was pointed out in the section on integration in the Civil Service.

Towards the end of World War II the 'évolués' (educated Africans) demanded that the administration should consult them before enforcing important decisions concerning Africans.

It was once more M. Robert Godding, the liberal Minister who was in charge of the Colonial Office immediately after World War II, who began to put an end to the white monopoly, at least in the various advisory councils of the time. The first step in this direction was the establishment of an elaborate labour organisation in which workers' representatives could play an active role.

In 1947 the first African delegates joined the government and provincial councils;[1] gradually their number increased to eight in the government council and six in the provincial councils. In 1956 six of the eight Congolese delegates represented the traditional authorities and two were 'évolués'; in most of the provinces, the traditional authorities had at least half of the six seats reserved for Congolese representatives, the only exception being the Kasai Province, where the 'évolués' held five of the six Congolese seats. The middle classes and workers' leaders were very scantily represented on the provincial councils; one representative of the middle class held a seat in the Kasai, while a trade school instructor represented the working class in the Equator Province. These African councillors were nominated by the Governor-General or the provincial governor without any consultation.

In 1957 the composition of these councils was entirely changed and the new categories of councillors consisted of representatives of social, economic and cultural groups or associations, such as notables, employers, wage-earners, rural areas, urban areas and cultural associations. The Governor-General and the provincial governors nominated

[1] In 1948 there were still no African representatives in the provincial councils of the two settler provinces of Katanga and Kivu.

these councillors after consulting the groups and associations involved, but no elections were held. In each category the delegates could be African or European; the result was that in certain provinces the number of African councillors increased to one-third of the total.

About the same time councils were also created at *territoire* level; in them Africans at first formed either a large minority or a small majority; after the territorial elections of December 1959 they had a dominant majority.

The Congolese were also represented on the advisory boards set up by the Central Government for special purposes. The *Commission pour la Protection des Indigènes*, which was responsible for suggesting to the administration improvements in social and material living conditions throughout the territory, included four Congolese among its eighteen members in 1956.

The thirteen regional committees of the Native Welfare Fund (*Fonds du Bien-Etre Indigène*) included twenty-four Congolese in 1954, eleven of whom belonged to the urban educated class, while thirteen came from rural areas. As this body was set up to promote the material and moral development of traditional native society in the Belgian Congo and Rwanda-Burundi, it seemed appropriate to give considerably wider representation to the Congolese directly affected by such developments, that is to say those from rural areas. Consequently in the new councils appointed at the beginning of 1957, fifty-eight seats were held by Congolese representing rural communities, fifty-two belonging to the traditional *élite* and six to the new intellectual *élite*.

Finally the Congolese also took part in the work of the advisory committees of the African Settlements Board (*Office des Cités Africaines*) and of the central and regional savings banks, and the district and provincial advisory committees for the award of the *carte du mérite civique* (see p. 24). But on all these bodies they remained in a minority.

To what extent did this system of representation spring from a clearly defined policy and not just vague tendencies? Certainly the Belgian administration was already aware in

1946 that it should consider a programme of political emancipation for the future, and Governor-General Petillon
established in 1952 as a general principle that the new
institutions which had to be created should have their roots
in the existing political and administrative institutions. By
this he meant the *chefferies*, *secteurs*, *territoires*, districts,
provinces and general government. His idea was simply to
democratise all these administrative levels by giving them
elected councils.

So there were two movements contributing to the building of the future Congo nation. The Congolese-inspired
movement we mentioned in the previous section: it wanted
to build up local government units at a higher level which
would gradually replace the lower levels of central administration, namely the *territoires* and the districts. It was an
upward movement from below, from the people, an at-
tempt to infiltrate peacefully, but systematically, into the
higher levels of government. It was supposed that as this
happened the central government would gradually with-
draw from its positions and surrender them to the local
government movement. In the eyes of the Africans such a
move would have been tantamount to a real national
revolution, winning for them some form of internal autonomy, similar to that which the natives of French Equatorial
and West Africa acquired by the 'loi cadre' of 23 June
1956. It was this kind of autonomy that the *Abako* was asking
for in its memorandum of August 1956.

The Belgian administration preferred to encourage the
slow democratisation of the institutions of central government by granting more deliberative powers to the advisory
councils, committees and boards and also by gradually
increasing the number of Africans in these councils. In
this way the administration hoped to secure a peaceful
transition to greater autonomy at the higher government
levels, the existing territorial boundaries were maintained
and a strong centralised authority continued to be exercised
from Leopoldville. Even when forced, after the riots of
January 1959, to accelerate political emancipation, the

Belgian administration kept stubbornly to these principles, in order to maintain the political unity of the Congo.

Training of Leaders

The achievement of a full and effective participation by the Congolese in local as well as in the Central Government was only possible if national leaders were available. And the main charge made against Belgium by international opinion is that she granted independence to the Congo without training leaders capable of managing the country competently.

We have pointed out already that although elementary education was fairly well developed, secondary, technical and higher education had been to some extent neglected. Thus many Congolese were deprived of the opportunity to acquire the knowledge and ability which might bring them the same chances of promotion as Europeans.

The need to train national leaders had, however, been perfectly understood in the early twenties by the far-sighted liberal Minister, Louis Franck. His plan of creating administrative services within the framework of the *chefferies* and the *secteurs*, in order to turn them into a type of municipal government, could have succeeded only if there had been leaders capable of commanding, directing and advising the new institutions.

M. Franck therefore gave directions for the organisation of a system of education for the chiefs and the traditional dignitaries and also for their heirs, so that they could learn to fulfil properly the various functions entrusted to them under the new regulations, and to control the registers, account-books and other documents involved in the new system.

M. Franck's views were shared by the Vicar Apostolic of the Kwango, who wrote in 1923 in a memorandum on general principles of colonial policy: 'The natural chiefs can only become the leaders in the work of spiritual and economic rescue of the populations they command, if they are duly educated.'

The first school for the sons of chiefs, directed by missionaries, was set up at Buta (Eastern Province); others were founded in other provinces, including one at Saint-Antoine, near Lusambo, but the system was given up on the futile pretext that it was unwise to take the sons of the chiefs out of their traditional environment.

M. Vermeulen, honorary district commissioner, gives the real reason for the abandonment of Franck's plan:

'It must be considered that most of the candidate-chiefs were sons of polygamists and likely to follow the example of their father on their return to the village. This was so true that the Fathers were reluctant to baptise the sons of chiefs. This can be easily understood. A school managed by Fathers, entrusted with the education of future polygamists, was hardly conceivable.'[1]

The system was given up in about 1929. It ought to have been replaced by another training-system, directed by civil servants, but it was not. The Catholic Ministers of Colonies who succeeded M. Franck showed little interest in the training of national leaders.

The Governors and district commissioners unanimously regretted the decision to do away with the schools for chiefs' sons, because the experiment proved later on to have been a success and when they were called to take over from their fathers or uncles the young men who had received their education in these institutions showed themselves to be very competent leaders, possessing a good knowledge of their office and high moral qualities. The territorial and district officers repeatedly asked for these schools to be re-established in order to prepare the future native authorities and dignitaries and their auxiliaries to face the ever-growing responsibilities of modern administration in the local government units.

M. Franck's idea was to be taken up again a quarter of a century later by another liberal Minister of Colonies, M.

[1] V. Vermeulen, *Déficiences et dangers de notre politique indigène* (Imprimerie I.M.A., 1953), p. 33.

Buisseret. In September 1955 three schools of administration were opened in three different provinces, and three more a year later. But a broader plan was adopted than before: it was thought desirable not to isolate future chiefs, but to bring them into contact with the intellectual *élite* of the country; for this reason the schools provided training not only for future chiefs, but for all young people who wanted to make a career in local government, in public administration, courts, co-operatives, mutual associations, fundamental education, or community development.

Civil servants who had in the past been trained in educational methods were appointed to the new schools of administration. Their success came up to expectations and registrations had to be limited to a manageable number by a rigorous system of selection.

Once more the Catholic hierarchy unfortunately disapproved of this move and launched a violent campaign against it, accusing the Minister of taking the education of the *élite* of the country away from the mission schools and creating 'Führerschulen' in the Nazi style.[1] Anxious to come to an agreement with the Social Christian opposition party on the whole problem of education, M. Buisseret sacrificed the administration schools after they had been in existence only two years. This political compromise was unanimously regretted by the Africans and by the Belgian civil servants, who worked alongside the local government institutions and knew how much they needed leaders.

Thus in 1957, three years before Independence, a very wise and liberal Minister was obliged, under pressure from the Catholic hierarchy, to close the institutions set up to train the leaders who were of vital importance to the immediate future of the Congo. This was certainly one of the biggest mistakes made by the Belgians at a most crucial moment in the history of the Congo. For this the colonial administration bears no responsibility, because as soon as the decision was taken to close the schools it asked the

[1] See *La Libre Belgique*, 1 June, 1955 'Quand le maître d' école crée l'école des maîtres'.

Minister to establish centres to speed up administrative training. But as we saw in the last chapter, a start was not made until 1959.

The Congolese had to be trained not only for local administration, but also for the higher levels of central administration. In January 1946 a proposal was made to open the Colonial University of Antwerp, now called the University Institute of Overseas Territories, to Congolese students, and to prepare young men from the Congo and Belgium together for a career of territorial administration. Such a common education could have created a mutual understanding between the future Congolese and Belgian civil servants of the Congo.[1] If this proposal had been accepted the first Congolese territorial administrators might have been appointed by about 1950 or 1951, and they would have had considerable experience before Independence. The Belgian metropolitan administration disagreed with this suggestion and did not allow the Academic Council of the Colonial University to relax its conditions of admission for African students.

In the coming years only the Catholic University of Louvain took Congolese students, because very often their admission into the other universities was discouraged by the colonial administration. A typical case was that of M. Justin Bomboko, Minister of Foreign Affairs of the Congo Republic at the time of writing, who in 1955 was prevented by the Governor-General from coming to Belgium to begin his studies at Brussels University; a categorical order from the Minister was needed to lift the ban.

The admission of Congolese students into Belgian universities was also restricted by the rigorous conditions of admission. Capable medical assistants were prevented from starting medical studies at a university because they had no knowledge of Greek and Latin; for the same reason others could not start legal studies. All these regulations,

[1] Georges Brausch, 'Pour des études coloniales spécialisées', Supplement au *Bulletin de l'Association des Anciens Etudiants de l'Université Coloniale de Belgique*, January 1946, p. 8.

which were logical in the Belgian educational context, were incomprehensible to the Congolese, who wondered why the secondary schools of their country were organised in such a way as to make admission to a university impossible.

Recently M. Langenhove, ex-permanent representative of Belgium at the United Nations, declared that the Congo's lack of university-trained leaders must be ascribed to the backward state of the native population.[1] This argument does not stand up to comparative investigation: French Equatorial Africa and Italian Somaliland, two countries which were certainly not more advanced than the Congo, had in 1957 562 and 1,140 students respectively being trained in the countries of the Common Market; these represent a proportion of 114 and 904 students respectively per million inhabitants. From the Congo at the same time there were less than a hundred students, a proportion of seven per million inhabitants. No excuse can be advanced for such backwardness in a country which was considered to be the richest in Africa after the Union of South Africa.

Only recently has the Belgian Government reacted to the situation. In January 1961 about 450 Congolese students were being educated on government bursaries at Belgian universities or higher institutes. Unfortunately these measures came much too late.

Community Development

Real democracy means full participation by the population in the management not only of political but also of economic and social matters.

The integration of the population into schemes of economic and social development must, in order to cover the whole country, be achieved simultaneously in both the industrial and the rural spheres. In a previous section we showed how the Congolese labour-organisation tried to give the wage-earners a fuller share in industrial and social

[1] F. van Langenhove, 'La crise congolaise: 1 janvier 1959–15 août 1960', *Chronique de Politique Etrangère* (Institut Royal des Relations Internationales), vol. XIII, nos. 4–6 (July–November 1960), p. 433.

development schemes. Similar steps need to be taken in the rural areas. But the integration of the rural population into schemes of economic and social development can be successfully achieved only at a local level, in the *commune*, the small township, the village or any other corresponding unit, whatever its name may be. It is therefore called 'community development'. In the Congo such steps need to be taken at local government level in the *chefferies* and *secteurs*.

While on the one hand the methods of community development can greatly facilitate economic and social progress and direct it towards the real need of the local communities, economic and social progress can stimulate community activities and develop the collective and individual initiative of the inhabitants. So the methods of community development are used to help the population to contribute to its own economic and social progress.

For some years the Belgian colonial administration worked out schemes of economic development in certain rural areas. They were known as 'paysannats indigènes' (farm settlement schemes). But the initiative and the responsibility for the execution of these schemes were left entirely in the hands of the Belgian administration, and the role of the African rural communities remained strictly that of obedient performers; consequently an important element necessary to community development was lacking.

Community development as a means of economic and social progress was limited in the Congo to a few experiments[1] in which the government departments showed little interest. Consequently these experiments did not become widespread, even when they were successful.

Nevertheless there were elements in the Congo that were favourable to successful community development work, chief among them a population which claimed to be ready

[1] An example can be seen in the social activities in the township of Ruashi at Elisabethville described by Mlle. Yvette Pirlot in a report of September 1959: '*Une expérience d'action sociale dans milieu urbain du Congo Belge*' (duplicated by the Solvay Centre of Social Research in Katanga).

to take an active share in the development schemes for their own communities.

Although the Belgian higher colonial administration was not always conscious of the need to give more freedom of initiative and responsibility to the local units in matters of economic development, we must admit that there was always keen interest in this problem among the chiefs of the *chefferies* and the *secteurs*, and the burgomasters of the *communes*: it is not generally known how constantly these authorities referred to the Belgian territorial administrators, with petitions for agricultural machines, schools, dispensaries, water supplies, lighting, roads, etc.

While these people insistently demanded that the Government should show some interest in their prosperity, they also made sure that they themselves were ready to take part collectively and individually in the execution of the development schemes which concerned them.

A second stimulus to community development work was a strongly organised system of local government, which is the natural framework of a community development scheme, and a fairly elaborate equipment of community institutions in the economic and social field. The village *panchayat* in India, the *barrio* council in the Philippines, the *mura* in Japan and the *desa* in Indonesia are all examples of successful co-ordination of local government units with community development programmes.[1] And the grave difficulties which are encountered by Egypt and Ethiopia in their development schemes must be ascribed to the absence in both countries of democratic local government units. In Egypt a Republican Decree of 26 March 1960 decided on the creation of such institutions as an indispensable tool for their future development plans, but the authorities agree that it may take a generation before they work efficiently; people must first get accustomed to them, and that may need some years of education.

[1] *Public Administration Aspects of Community Development Programmes*, United Nations Technical Assistance Programmes (New York, 1959), pp. 47–59.

We have already pointed out that in the Congo, on the other hand, such local government units have existed since 1891 and that they were gradually endowed with embryonic administrative units. We remember too that this transformation was completed by the Decree of 10 May 1957, which established a system of popular consultation for the constitution of the councils of those units and that most of them possess a fairly elaborate infrastructure of departments and institutions. In each case these existing bodies could have been an excellent starting-point from which to launch a future community development programme.

A third circumstance favourable to community development work in the Congo was the existence of a staff of well trained officers, knowing the country and the people, who might have been easily converted into community development experts.

Although the term 'community development' is of recent date, we must not hastily conclude that the methods which come under this heading are completely new. It is beyond doubt that the patient efforts of certain colonial administrators to help the local units to function better and to promote their economic and social progress belong strictly to the field of community development. Certainly too many of these colonial administrators resorted in the past to compulsion in their attempts to improve the living conditions of the native population, but we know that even in autonomous territories there is a strong temptation to do the same.

Certain less developed territories have therefore decided, instead of creating a brand new service with people with no experience of African administrative bodies or of the African people, to appeal to ex-district or territorial officers to join the community development staff.

Naturally certain preliminary conditions must be accepted: the officers transferred from the Civil Service must get used to the specific philosophy of their new service. That means that they must stop giving orders to the local communities and instead help and advise them. This change was managed most successfully in Ghana, Uganda and Kenya, where ex-district officers became community development officers.

A similar change might have been brought about in the Congo if the colonial administration had achieved the creation of a community development scheme in time, and if the tragic events of July and August 1960 had not upset all plans.

A last factor which could have greatly stimulated community development in the Belgian territories in Africa was the existence of various agencies committed to development work, which might have been converted into community development agencies without any great difficulty.

Under the colonial rule certain aspects of development work were indeed entrusted to the care of para-state agencies, acting independently of government agencies. Two of the most typical of these were the Native Welfare Fund (*Fonds du Bien-Etre Indigène*) and the Special Committee of the Katanga.

The Native Welfare Fund was created by a Decree signed by Charles the Prince Regent at Leopoldville on 1 July 1947 during a visit to Africa. To it were entrusted all plans bearing on the material and moral development of the traditional native society in the Belgian Congo and Ruanda-Urundi.

Again, as we have already noted, the councils and committees which had to decide on the programmes were composed mostly of Europeans, with few Africans, while the interested rural communities themselves were considered insufficiently mature to be consulted about the plans being made for their well-being. It was not until 1957 that, by Minister Buisseret's decision, a larger number of rural Africans began to sit in the consultative councils of the Native Welfare Fund, but they were in a minority. The Minister moreover decreed that every new project should also be submitted first to the councils of the interested local government units (*chefferies* or *secteurs*).

Notwithstanding these liberal measures—which were considered revolutionary at the time—we cannot say that up to Independence the Fund came near to real community development, as the essential elements were missing, namely the free initiative and responsibility of the people as regards proposals as well as execution.

The Special Committee of the Katanga was a chartered society created in 1901 to deal with land management and development in the province. Its task included the economic development of the region but not the management of 'native land', which was thus excluded from its development schemes. Over a period of sixty years the agency succeeded in making very elaborate and interesting studies of the potential agricultural and industrial development of the Katanga.

With the approach of Independence it was suggested that the activities of this agency should be extended to the 'native land' and that it should be converted into a 'Special Committee for Community Development in the Katanga', which would inherit the rich documentation of its predecessor and use it to launch a large programme of economic and social progress for the African communities.

In spite of all these favourable circumstances the higher levels of the Belgian colonial administration were not prepared to accept the idea of community development, and opposed all the directions and suggestions which were made in this field, even if they came directly from the Minister. In 1955 and 1956 Minister Buisseret instructed the Governor-General of the Belgian Congo to institute a general enquiry into the launching of community development work. But as the colonial administration was not convinced of the necessity of the proposed methods, it presented no positive proposals confining itself to criticisms and tergiversations.

Even at the approach of Independence the higher authorities refused to adopt a more realistic attitude towards community development. This field was seriously neglected both at the Round Table Conference of January and February 1960, and at the Economic Conference of April and May 1960 which laid down the conditions of economic co-operation between the Congo and Belgium. Neither of these conferences went beyond general economic considerations, or conceived any economic planning except on the national, company or trade union levels, considering the level of the local communities to be accessory if not negligible. They did not realise the importance of local government institutions in instigating a popular momentum among the mass of the population toward economic and social progress.

Aware that the Belgian Government was either not willing or else not able to support such a scheme, the General Executive College[1] asked the International Co-operation Administration to send a delegation to study methods for the development of Congolese local communities. This was done in April and May 1960 and an agricultural extension scheme was planned, but because of the prevailing political conditions, nothing was done about it.

Owing to the shortcomings of the colonial administration, the Government of the Congo Republic found itself in July 1960 faced with the whole burden of launching from nothing a development plan for the economic and social progress of the local communities.

---

[1] The General Executive College was a board of seven, exercising supreme administrative powers in the Belgian Congo from the end of the Round Table Conference to Independence Day. It was composed of the Governor-General and six African members, one for each province, appointed by delegates to the Round Table Conference.

IV. BREAKTHROUGH TO
INDEPENDENCE

WE started this account by observing the great benefits brought to the Congo by its mineral wealth. This made possible a rapid industrialisation and consequently a high national income in which the Africans shared, as wage-earners or by selling their agricultural products, and also an elaborate system of social institutions. Certainly there were great differences between the African and European ways of life, but the Government took care that certain discriminatory measures which had been enforced to protect the Africans did not become vexatious and as soon as they were no longer needed they were gradually abolished.

In the chapter on the participation of the Africans in government we mentioned that local government was always completely African. But there were serious shortcomings in the Congolese system, in particular the insufficient representation of Africans in central government, the lack of training of Africans for leadership and the failure to bring about active participation by the Congolese in the social and economic development schemes which directly concerned them.

But can we say that these few faults were sufficiently important to neutralise completely all the favourable elements we have mentioned? Certainly not. Other factors contributed to the collapse of the Congo and we shall try to bring them out in this chapter.

Belgian Ignorance and Misapprehensions about the Congo

For years the Belgians, the man in the street as well as the political leaders, took very little interest in African affairs. The average Belgian has never been imperialistically minded and he did not bother much about the African territories administered by his country. Even the Belgian politicians did not give them much thought; for instance, the Minister of Colonies generally made his annual report on African affairs to a nearly empty Parliament. Consequently there were many false ideas in Belgium about the Congo. *The Belgian man in the street* knew little about what was going on in Central Africa; he ignored the great social, economic and even political changes which were occurring and continued to think in terms of a barbarous Africa inhabited by savages.

Great was the astonishment of the bulk of the Belgian population when, at the invitation of the Minister of Colonies, the first groups of Africans visited Belgium and it was discovered that those 'native' visitors were well-educated and courteous people, speaking French correctly, easily understanding what was explained to them and showing a good cultural background. The shock was the greater as the first of these visitors was the lordly and spectacular figure of Mwami Mutara Rudahigwa of Rwanda.

At once the Belgians went to the other extreme; forgetting that these people had been invited because they were the most distinguished of their countrymen, because they were an *élite*, they could not understand why all the Congo people had not been given more civic rights in their country. And when clashes occurred in Leopoldville in January 1959, the astonishment of the Belgian people grew quickly into indignation and Belgian colonials who were in Belgium at that time were accused of being imperialists, profiteers, exploiters; in some cases their cars were stoned. While the term 'colonial' acquired a pejorative meaning, the 'coloniaux' invented the nickname 'Belgicains' for their metropolitan compatriots, whom they accused of not wanting to understand the real nature of the situation in Central Africa. Thus a real rift developed between the 'Belgicains' and the 'coloniaux'.

Belgian politicians discovered the Congo in 1947, when a commission of the Belgian Senate paid a visit of several

weeks, to investigate the situation in the overseas territories
and to make recommendations for future policy. The report
which was published after the visit contains information
about general administration, demography, justice, transport, public health, economics, as well as a remarkable
report (by far the most detailed section, fifty pages long) by
M. Buisseret on education; special sections were devoted
to the settlers, the Eurafricans and the indigenous and
white workers. But little attention or none was given to
such important items as native administration, the training
of leaders, the problem of the *élites*, human relations, the
political advancement of the Africans, the economic and
social progress of the local communities, fundamental
education, housing and the promotion of an African
middle class.

During their journey many of these politicians were more
concerned about their Belgian voters than about the great
colonial problems of the moment; the Social Christian
Senators made a point of visiting Catholic missionaries and
stayed away from the Protestant mission stations, while the
Socialists showed a particular interest in the white wage-
earners.

Later more and more politicians came to the Congo and
they showed a growing interest in African problems, but
unfortunately the judgment of many of them was tainted
with Western prejudices. They envisaged the future evolution of African society on an ethnocentric pattern, as a
perfect reproduction of the Western prototype of industrial
and democratic revolution, and they were convinced that
the values, as well as the attitudes and the motivations of
Western civilisation should be instilled, along with Western
techniques.

Nevertheless some differences could be observed between the views of the various parties. The Social Christians
considered that the overseas territories ought to develop
towards becoming a Christian state, obeying Christian
principles; and that African traditional institutions and
African chiefs were relics of a paganism which had to be

extirpated; consequently they declared that old institutions and the traditional authorities were no longer suited to modern conditions and suggested that new institutions should be substituted, with statutes based upon the Social Christian doctrines and directed by an intellectual *élite*, educated in Catholic schools; in the next section we shall show how this policy was enforced between 1948 and 1954.[1]

The Socialists professed to be more flexible; just as they have adapted their Marxist doctrine to the Western mentality, they were ready to do the same in Central Africa in order to reconcile their principles with the African philosophy and the African political and social structure. In fact, however, the Socialists showed themselves to be categorically opposed to African traditionalism, which in their view expressed a primitive and old-fashioned feudalism; they could not agree to the maintenance of customary chiefs, drawing their power from hereditary and aristocratic rights or wealth; socialist syndicalism was also opposed to the corporate nature of African tribal life.

The Liberals showed more comprehension of African society; they considered that African philosophy and the African political and social structure should serve as a basis for the future development of that society; liberal policy consisted principally in helping the Africans to the full to adapt their institutions to new contingencies, but in their view these adaptations should not necessarily be achieved in accordance with European principles, but might follow African patterns. MM. Franck, Godding and Buisseret adhered to this policy when they were in charge of the Ministry of Colonies.

[1] The spokesman for this policy was Professor G. Malengreau of the University of Louvain; he stated these opinions in a written answer to suggestions by different Belgian personalities about 'La formation politique des indigènes congolais', organised by *Problèmes d'Afrique Centrale* in its issues nos. 13 and 14 (1951). The same year, in his encyclical *Evangelii Praecones*, Pope Pius XII insisted on the need to develop Catholic-inspired economic and social associations and institutions in missionary countries.

These differences of approach by the Belgian political parties to colonial policy were responsible for certain vacillations after World War II.

Inconsistency of Belgian Colonial Policy

Four periods are distinguishable in Belgian colonial policy since World War II: 1945–1947: a period of social progress; 1947–1954: a period of assimilation; 1954–1958: a period of gradual emancipation; 1958–1960: a period of headlong emancipation.

Social Reforms (1945–1947).—Because of the lack of interest among the Belgian people and politicians in the problems of the Congo, the Belgian colonial administration —the Ministry of Colonies in Brussels as well as the general government departments in Leopoldville—was for years in a state of isolation; it was obliged to act alone, without any help from outside, and as everything seemed to be working very well it was not inclined to make revolutionary changes.

Immediately after World War II, from 1945 to 1947, a very sincere desire sprang up all over the world to advance colonial territories towards greater freedom. When M. Godding became Minister of Colonies in 1945, he intended to apply gradually the resolutions of the United Nations Charter with regard to the non-autonomous territories which had been adopted at the San Francisco Conference in 1945. He was responsible for the creation of a special section of Information and Propaganda for the Africans, which gave assistance and advice to African 'cercles' and clubs, created or encouraged the creation of African newspapers, arranged African radio and film programmes and encouraged the public expression of African opinion.

In January 1946 Minister Godding directed the Governor-General to issue the Ordinances on the organisation of labour for Africans (see pp. 15–16) imposing an obligatory system of works councils, local labour committees, commissions of labour and social progress, and authorising the creation of trade unions.

The same Minister prepared the plans for the foundation of an organised department of social assistance, of the *Fonds du Bien-Etre Indigène* and of the *Office des Cités Africaines*, but unfortunately he had to leave the Colonial Office before completing his projects, owing to a change of government in Belgium. His departure was unanimously regretted, by the Africans to whom he had given a glimpse of hope of more freedom, as well as by the Europeans, who had confidence in the wisdom of this quiet man who wanted to keep the Congo out of the political turmoil in Belgium.

Policy of Assimilation (1947–1954).—Minister Wigny, M. Godding's successor, started very wisely to carry out the projects mentioned above, but while M. Godding had a liberal structure in mind, with Africans participating fully in the work of the new institutions, his successor reverted to the old Belgian paternalistic pattern giving little or no initiative or responsibility to the Africans.

But those in power from 1948 to 1954 were obliged to make some response to the claims of the Congolese for fuller participation and it was they who devised the *carte du mérite civique* and the *immatriculation* of Africans, which after a long and vexatious enquiry into their private lives gave certain privileges, which very often remained theoretical, to the very tiny minority who were assimilated to European standards of life. The official attitude was that the Africans ought to merit their advance to European status, and that this advance should be achieved very slowly.

Besides these decrees, intended to hold out bright prospects to the Africans, there were others that attempted to force the mass of the population into a European, Christian way of life, for instance by the abolition of polygamy, the protection of monogamy, the proscription of certain traditional associations which secured the maintenance of pagan rituals, and likewise of the autonomous Christian churches such as Kibangism and Kitawala which tried to respond to spiritual aspirations which the older-established churches could not fully satisfy. According to the Social

Christian doctrine, this policy aimed at preparing the way for a Congolese State loyal to the Church, where the priests would be the shepherds of the population.

In fact the period from 1947 to 1954 was one of little movement; the progressive policy of M. Godding had been halted and this immobilism was encouraged unconsciously by international public opinion, which praised to the skies the wise policy of Belgium, often making things difficult for certain people and groups at home, who were demanding a long-range political programme for the future.

Gradual Emancipation (1954–1958).—The 1954 elections in Belgium brought into power a liberal-socialist coalition Government and a liberal Colonial Minister, who decided to go on with the progressive programme started by M. Godding. Compared with the previous years a great deal was achieved during this four-year period.

Greater freedom of speech and of publication was allowed as long as public order was not endangered; in the field of public administration new Royal Decrees provided for the fuller democratisation of local government institutions in both rural and urban areas, and the Africans were given a fuller share in the various institutions which directly concerned them; the powers and prestige of the African authorities were strengthened; the social assistance services were developed, the number of social centres was doubled and new methods of social action were inaugurated; all forms of racial discrimination were gradually eliminated; full freedom of association, and specifically of association in trade unions, was granted; more progressive social security and insurance legislation gave African labour most of the social advantages to be found in the more highly-developed countries; the whole educational system was developed and integrated and two universities were founded.

The coalition Government would have liked to do more, but even these innovations were given an unfriendly reception by the conservatives. The latter had the complete support of the opposition party of the moment, which thought only of its short-term electoral interests and not of the interests of the Congo and the Belgian future in the Congo. Thus, for fear of being regarded as extremists, supporters of Communism and the grave-diggers of the Belgian nation, a very liberal and far-sighted Government was obliged to moderate its programme of emancipation for the Congo at a most crucial moment.

Looking back at this period now, after Independence, we must admit that in view of what was going to happen, this very progressive policy was still too timid. I use the word 'timid' with full knowledge of the facts, because from 1954 to 1957 I was myself an adviser on political and social affairs on the staff of the Ministry of Colonies and I am fully aware that during this period we were too slow in introducing the innovations which were needed for the months to come.

No Timetable for Independence

Although the political parties were the first means by which the Africans could express their demands for independence, the idea had never been absent from their minds since the Belgians occupied the country in 1879. It would be unrealistic to deny this; white people have always been regarded in the Congo as an occupying power in a conquered country. And although the Governor-General of the Congo admitted in 1952 that it was time to think about a programme of gradual political emancipation for the African population, the word 'independence' never appeared in his speeches. The idea of granting independence to the Congo in some far distant future was first expressed by Belgian statesmen in 1954, when the radical coalition Government came to power.

The first serious public demands for independence were, however, made in July and August 1956 in the manifestos of *Conscience Africaine* and of *Abako*, and at that time the most extreme nationalists talked in terms of a thirty-year plan, postponing complete independence to 1986. Wide of the mark as it was, this proposal was received at the time with real terror by the Belgians, in the Congo as well as in the mother-country.

The Minister of Colonies and the Governor-General both refused to respond to these manifestos with a concrete government plan; they regarded the proclamations as nonsense and even certain African political leaders thought —of course quite unrealistically—that Belgian rule would last another hundred years.

This was unrealistic because about that time internal autonomy was granted to the French territories in Africa by the 'loi cadre' of Minister Deferre and full independence was given to the Sudan and Ghana. We can see now how far the two very liberal Decrees democratising African local government lagged behind what was going on in the neighbouring territories.

Thus 1956 appears in the history of the Congo as a dangerous turning-point. In that year the Belgian colonial administration, which till then had always kept ahead of social and political claims, was passed by them, and would never catch them up again. No reply was given to the manifestos of *Conscience Africaine* and *Abako*; claims of 'equal pay for equal work' were shelved and only granted three years later.

This was certainly a great mistake for a very progressive Government but, as we mentioned before, this political timidity was brought about by the uncomprehending attitude of a narrow-minded opposition party, which refused to understand that certain problems of national importance needed to be examined apart from all electoral preoccupations. Instead the Social Christian politicians appealed to public opinion with striking slogans which were very harmful to the reputation of the Government, representing very moderate innovations as having a revolutionary character. This was a dangerous game, because public opinion is very inconsistent and as quick to become indignant at the supposed threat of losing colonial territories, as at the misdoings of the white colonialists. The strong pressure of such opinion prevented the Government from achieving further innovations.

1956 was also the year of the economic recession in the United States of America, and as the economy of the Congo was very dependent upon that of the U.S., this recession was felt there more deeply than in other countries.

At the same time it was decided that because of the fall in financial resources social projects which were not directly productive should be halted. Among these was the scheme for economic and social advancement in the rural areas by the methods of community development, which were wrongly presented by certain conservatives as being Communist or Marxist inspired.

So of the three pillars of the Congolese structure, *economic prosperity*, *social progress* and *local administration*, two were badly undermined. The last alone retained its strength.

The 1958 elections brought a new change in the Belgian political field; a Socialist Christian Government again came into power and the Governor-General, M. Petillon, accepted the Ministry of Colonies, but changed its title to 'Ministry of the Belgian Congo and Ruanda-Urundi'. He decided on a policy of 'decolonisation' and appointed a parliamentary commission, to make an enquiry in the Congo with a view to formulating a policy of emancipation. This decision took the initiative and the responsibility for the management of the country away from the Belgian authorities in the Congo and surrendered its destiny to the Belgian politicians. From now on every decision by an authority in the Congo, every event, was subject to discussion in Belgium; as a reaction the Congo authorities would refer the smallest decision to their superiors and consequently the administrative machinery seized up.

Meanwhile political unrest had started to develop and culminated in the riots of January 1959 in Leopoldville, before any programme for political emancipation had been announced. On 13 January 1959, nine days after the beginning of the riots, the Belgian Government at last announced a decision; but the speed with which ideas had developed in two and a half years was shown by the fact that what it now proposed was a five-year plan.

This was accepted at first by all the political parties, except the *Abako*, but was rejected in June by the 'Memorandum of the Eight' (the eight most important political parties at the time), which demanded independence in 1961. Immediately after that M. Lumumba's *Mouvement National Congolais* asked for independence in June 1960.

In order to come to an agreement with the political leaders, the Belgian Government organised a Round Table Conference in January and February 1960 at which 45 Congolese political leaders met the mandated delegates of the Belgian Government and the three Belgian traditional parties. The decision was taken to grant complete independence on 30 June 1960. The thirty-year plan had shrunk to nothing and in fact no timetable governed the transition of the Congo from a colony to an independent state .

The Belgian political leaders, who had been worried in 1956, 1957 and 1958 by the deterioration in the economic situation, completely lost confidence in the future of the Congo after the tragic events of January 1959. Entirely overwhelmed by these events, they were unable—as was the Belgian colonial administration too—to think out a sound plan of decolonisation; when they had a plan, they lacked the courage to put it into operation and retreated before the demands of the first Congolese leader who opposed them.

Breakdown of Authority

African Authority.—The principle of authority has always been sacred in African society, because it was associated with paternal power. The patriarch of the kinship group, the master of the workshop, the leader of a magico-political society or the chief of a tribe were respected and venerated by those who were dependent upon them, not because they were feared, but because they protected them by their authority as the father protects his children. The man who was feared was regarded as an enemy and not as a leader.

When the Belgians penetrated into Central Africa, they recognised the African traditional institutions with their whole hierarchy of authorities; but during the years which followed they curtailed many of their powers and, through ignorance, often transgressed against the rules of respect due toward chiefs. But the chiefs' authority was safeguarded by the fact that they still exercised their traditional powers, though in a diminished form, in the new circumstances and kept their dominant position among their kinsmen.

The successive Decrees of 1891, 1906, 1910 and 1933 recognised the chiefs as the cornerstone of native administration; they were indeed the spokesmen for their tribesmen to the colonial administration and they also ensured that decisions of the colonial administration were carried out in their districts. This task was not easy as they very often had to reconcile sharply conflicting points of view; nevertheless they succeeded fairly well because they were listened to as wise and venerated leaders.

It was in about 1943 that certain progressive Belgians started to criticise the system; they accused the chiefs of being feudalists, fossilised conservatives, keeping their subjects in a backward state and incapable of adapting themselves to modern contingencies. This campaign against the chiefs was conducted at first by Mgr. de Hemptinne of Elisabethville and a group of young Belgian Catholics, who advocated the substitution of young 'évolués' for the traditional chiefs.[1]

[1] M. Antoine Rubbens, an Elisabethville barrister, collected in a book, under the title *Dettes de guerre* (Elisabethville, Les Cahiers de la Politique Indigène, 1945), a series of articles published by these young Catholics during the years 1944 and 1945 in the newspaper *L'Essor du Congo*.   The feelings of the group towards the traditional chiefs appears for instance on p. 25, where Rubbens blames the 'decrepitude of the chiefs' and the 'venality of the judges' and on p. 47, where he calls the chiefs 'useless puppets, whose right place is in a folk-museum' and accuses them 'of committing all sorts of exactions and abuses'. On p. 31, one of the writers, P.G., speaking of the traditional judges, calls them 'a gang of leeches'.

This point of view was adopted by the Social Christian Party and from 1947 to 1954 their Ministers favoured this policy; however the young educated chiefs found it very difficult to impose their authority, because they did not possess the traditional prestige; at the same time great damage was done to the authority of the traditional chiefs. Various eminent colonial personalities and administrators saw the danger of this deterioration of authority and they warned the higher colonial administration of the detrimental consequences it might have on the maintenance of law and order.[1]

Minister Buisseret tried to re-establish the authority of the chiefs by improving their material situation, giving them a higher status, inviting them to important national ceremonies, arranging visits and study tours for them, increasing their participation in different advisory boards, founding schools of administration for the training of future chiefs and especially by increasing their powers at local government level. All these measures were much appreciated by the mass of the population and even by the educated *élite*, who were delighted at this restoration of value to their national institutions.[2]

The Social Christian Opposition Party again seized this occasion to blame the Minister for encouraging pagan

[1] Louis Dekoster, 'Le chef indigène', *Revue Général Belge*, no. 43, May 1949, pp. 143–8.
Jean Paelinck, 'Les autorités indigènes', *Bulletin de l'Association des Anciens Etudiants de l'Institut Universitaire des Territoires d'Outre Mer*, 1950, no. 10.
Georges Moulaert, 'La formation politique des indigènes congolais', *Problèmes d'Afrique Centrale*, 4th year, no. 13, pp. 169–85.
V. Vermeulen, *Déficiences et dangers de notre politique indigène* (Brussels, Imprimerie I.M.A., 1953).
[2] M. Alois Kabangi, Minister of Planning and Economic Co-ordination in the Lumumba and Ileo Governments, has always been a great defender of the authority of the traditional chiefs; on the occasion of a visit to Belgium in 1955 he handed over to the Minister of Colonies a petition in favour of the chiefs; this document was used as a guide in the months to come in attempts to satisfy the demands it contained.

institutions, and at the same time it conducted a widespread campaign in its newspapers against the traditional authorities, accusing them of abuses, corruption, extortion, even of ritual murders. Many chiefs tried to take action against these charges and asked permission to open legal proceedings, but they were not allowed to because the administration feared an open conflict between the chiefs and the missionaries who published these newspapers. This was the beginning of a movement of civic disobedience, which spread rapidly over the whole Congo and found enthusiastic support among the youth of the country.

A typical example of the catastrophic consequences of such uncontrolled campaigns, based on slogans of Christian equality, is seen in Rwanda. There the Hutu were inoculated with a revolutionary virus, as dangerous as any Communist propaganda and with the same aim—the complete elimination of the Tutsi, the traditional aristocracy of the country.

The campaign was started in the early fifties in the *Temps Nouveaux d'Afrique*, a French weekly published in Usumbura by the White Fathers, and *Kinyameteka*, a fortnightly paper published in the Kinyarwanda language at Kabgay, the residence of the vicar apostolic of Rwanda. Week after week these publications made accusations undermining the authority of the Tutsi chiefs, who had served the Belgian missionaries and administrators loyally for years. At the same time emotional writings popularised the picture of an oppressed and exploited Hutu, who ought to be freed from the burdens of Tutsi slavery.

That the Hutu formed the proletariat of Rwanda was only partly true, because in spite of the obligations which linked him to his Tutsi master, he managed his affairs independently. Besides, many clear-sighted Tutsi, and among them Mwami Mutara Rudahigwa, agreed that the Hutu should be freed from their obligations; in 1953, the 'ubuhake' system, a traditional form of cattle *métayage*, was abolished by an order in council of the Mwami and the Hutu were entitled to become cattle proprietors; a similar reform for the system of land tenure was examined by the Superior Council of the country.

The higher trusteeship authorities openly encouraged the Hutu after the death of Mwami Mutara Rudahigwa, particularly when the dissatisfied Tutsi created a nationalist movement which demanded independence. The antagonism grew and culminated in 1959 in sanguinary slaughters between two opposed groups. All this might have been avoided if the attitude of certain administrators and officials and missionaries had been more impartial.

European Authority.—Those responsible for the breakdown of African authority do not seem to have been aware that their action undermined the whole principle of 'authority' in all its aspects and consequently of European authority too. The Africans very quickly extended to their European rulers the critical attitude and civic disobedience they had adopted towards their chiefs, just as in the past they had extended to the Belgian administrator, employer and missionary the filial respect and veneration they had for their traditional authorities. But the condition then was that the white man treated them in the traditional, customary way, that he gave them his protection; the white man who did not behave like a father, who showed no kindness, who gave no protection, was not obeyed.

The Africans have always respected and listened to Europeans who consented to live near to them, tried to understand them, talked to them and discussed their problems and used their wisdom to solve them. Ministers like MM. Franck and Buisseret, strong personalities who consented to sit informally at the same table with Africans and displayed interest in their problems, enjoyed a great popularity and were regarded as great white leaders.

On the other hand the Africans despised the white men of the towns, who showed themselves to be superior and peevish, who did not even know the native settlement next door to them, who admitted no contradiction when they spoke. Unfortunately the Congo and Rwanda-Burundi were governed in these last years mostly by bureaucrats, who had little or no practical knowledge of local administration and the problems of the mass of the population, and were guided only by juridical principles or economic theories.

Consequently it is not astonishing that when on 4 January 1960 the riots started in Leopoldville, no high personality, apart from the *Procureur du Roi*, had the courage to cope with the situation on the spot; instead they shut themselves up in their homes, protected by the military.

On that day the Africans discovered that the leaders of the white men were afraid of the black men, and this was to be confirmed by the policy of systematic abdication in the months to come. *So died the myth of the strength of the white man* and with it vanished all the confidence in his wisdom acquired by the African in the past.

Deterioration of African Confidence

Although the Belgians had given no immediate response to the manifestos of July and August 1956, the Africans and their emerging political leaders maintained a great confidence in the future during the following months.

M. Kasavubu wrote in all sincerity in the March 1957 issue of the Leopoldville monthly *La Voix du Congolais*:

'As to our co-operation with the Europeans, it must remain traditional. A tradition which must be full of humanity and charity.

'The first European who set foot on Congolese soil was welcomed with friendship by our ancestors. With the same hospitality it is customary to receive Congolese of another clan, another country, another racial grouping . . . As for us, we shall not deviate from this traditional behaviour of our ancestors. We shall practise their policy of living in peace, respecting the rights of the inhabitants. But we ask that our rights shall also be respected.'

About the same time M. Patrice Lumumba wrote with his well-known impetuosity:

'We rely with optimism on the good faith of the Belgian Government and are convinced that no effort will be neglected, either by the Belgians, or by the native *élites*, to facilitate and hasten the evolution of the indigenous populations towards autonomy.

'Autonomy or union, that is a question for the future. When we have enough African doctors, agricultural engineers, technicians, civil engineers, contractors, geologists, administrators, magistrates, only then can we ask that question.

'For the present and for years to come, we have no desire to separate from the Belgians, as there are no reasons at present to justify such a separation.

'We must still get it into our heads that in the Congo, without the Blacks the Whites are of no value and without the Whites the Blacks have no value either. This economic interdependence makes union necessary for us.

'In the same way, we fight against all racialism or selfish nationalism, because such feelings generate social conflicts. Our dearest wish—perhaps some may find it utopian—is to found in the Congo a Nation in which differences of race and religion will melt away, a homogeneous society composed of Belgians and Congolese, who with a single impulse will link their hearts to the destinies of the country. It is only at the price of such common effort that we shall succeed in safeguarding our freedom and our national unity.'[1]

The fact that these sentences were written in jail by the future Prime Minister of the Congo Republic gives an even greater significance to them. In a memorandum, entitled *Le Congo, terre d'avenir, est-il menacé?*[2], finished about 21 January 1957, M. Lumumba devoted three hundred pages to celebrating Belgo-Congolese friendship. He repeated statements of this sort throughout the whole of that year and even in 1958 after leaving prison, for instance in April at a general meeting of the Atetela federation, when he was elected as their president.

[1] In a letter to the author.

[2] Published in Brussels, 1961, by Editions de l'Office de Publicité.

The Africans patiently awaited a decision on their claims for 'equal pay for equal work'; they knew that the negotiations were going ahead in spite of certain opposition, and finally the news came that a definite decision would be submitted to a final meeting of the delegates of the various interested parties. While the Africans expressed great satisfaction, the Europeans showed discontent, which was exploited once more by Minister Buisseret's political opponents. On his arrival at Elisabethville on 22 February 1958, angry settlers and even government officials organised a noisy demonstration to show their disagreement with the 'statut unique', which established equal conditions and salaries for all government employees, black and white. The African population disapproved of the behaviour of the Europeans and next day organised a demonstration of sympathy for the Minister.

This lack of sympathy among the white population of Elisabethville shook the confidence of many Africans; they came to the conclusion that the Europeans were not in favour of their advancement and that they would have to fight for any improvement in their situation. At the same time they were deeply shocked by the lack of courtesy among the whites towards their own authorities.

Their confidence received a new blow when a few months later Minister Buisseret, whom many regarded as a liberator, left the Ministry of Colonies. The installation of a conservative Government augured badly in the minds of the Africans, especially when the Colonial Office went to Governor-General Petillon, with whom the Africans had never felt much sympathy. Even this announced intention to follow a policy of 'decolonisation' could not stir up their enthusiasm, and when he visited Elisabethville in August 1958 the Africans paid him back for the white population's disrespectful demonstrations against Minister Buisseret six months earlier.

At that moment the Africans began to be uneasy and discontented at the growth of unemployment, which struck particularly at the young; those who were unemployed

quickly became delinquents and rebels. It was these young
people who organised the riots of 4 January 1959 in Leopoldville and who destroyed the schools to which they had
not been admitted because of lack of space; the riots of
Stanleyville of 29 October 1959 were also the work of
youngsters; even now these teenagers, for instance the
Jeunesses Baluba in North Katanga and the *Jeunesses M.N.C.*
in the Kivu Province, continue to cause disturbances in the
Congo Republic. These groups reject all authority and
create anarchy wherever they get the chance.

Events after January 1959 continued to undermine
African confidence in the Europeans, for instance the
cowardly behaviour of the Belgian high officials during the
riots and the continual vacillations and hesitations with
regard to the timing of independence. While in the past,
Belgian colonial policy had been characterised by the
slogan: *firmness and kindness*, in the last months of colonial
rule, all *firmness* was abandoned and *kindness* became weak-
ness.

The final blow was struck at the confidence of the
Africans by their political advisers. For years African associations had appealed to Europeans to help them in their
management and these whites had given their services in a
friendly and modest manner with no thought of honours or
reward, but with a sincere desire to help the Africans,
stimulated by a strong idealistic conception of the duties
of the white men in Africa. A great deal of the work of the
cultural associations, the social clubs, the organisation of
leisure and sports during the last years was the fruit of their
labour, and the Africans felt a great sympathy for these
advisers who day after day came to the African settlements
after work and sacrificed most of their leisure time to
welfare work. It was natural that the new political parties
at first asked for help from these advisers, but the latter
were inclined towards conciliation and moderation in
political action

In 1958 many of the emergent political leaders came to
Brussels, either as visitors or as employees at some stand at

the International Exhibition. They were enticed by young Belgian intellectuals (university professors, sociologists or barristers) who fancied themselves as cut out to play a role in the liberation of Central Africa; they convinced the African political leaders that the wise and moderate advice of their white friends in the Congo was inspired by an interested concern to prolong Belgian rule as long as possible, and that they could only advance rapidly towards freedom and independence with the help of a group of young Belgian intellectuals. These people appeared in public for the first time at the Round Table Conference of January and February 1960, where they were incorporated as official political advisers.

Instead of trying above all to express clearly, frankly and objectively, in all their simplicity, the basic opinions and demands of the African political group that had called upon them, the political advisers strove to capture their support for their own Belgian political parties and make them side with Western political, economic, financial, social and religious theories, in which the Congolese were not at all interested and saw no practical advantage for their group. Typical in this respect was the pressure exerted by the Social Christian Party upon the *Abako*, the *M.N.C.—Kalonji* (a dissident faction of M. Lumumba's party) and M. Bolikango's *Parti de l'Union Nationale* (*PUNA*), and by the Belgian Socialist Party upon the *Parti Solidaire Africain*, the *Parti Progressiste du Katanga* (*Balubakat*), the *Union des Mongo* and the *Parti du Peuple*.

At the same time these advisers wanted to make themselves useful to the Congolese party that they were backing, and they recommended electoral techniques used in Europe, with their whole battery of insults, calumnies, underhand blows and intrigues; according to newspaper reports a university professor even sent a team of his research staff to help in the electoral campaign of a group of political parties he was supporting personally.[1]

[1] *Le Soir*, 9 June; *L'Essor du Congo*, 13 June; *Le Courrier d'Afrique*, 10 June; *Pourquoi Pas?*, 8 July 1960.

The colonials did not want to lag behind and they also joined in the struggle, but as they gave their support to the more moderate parties, the latter were at once suspected of being sold to the whites and the capitalists and they lost popularity; the *P.N.P.* was the chief victim of this reaction.

All this resulted in great confusion, in which nobody, neither the Africans nor the Europeans, knew any longer what they were doing. Europeans were fighting and denouncing one another and trying to avenge themselves under the banners of the African political parties. The most scandalous case reported by the newspapers in this field was the suppression by the Katanga Government, allegedly on the advice of a Belgian university professor, of the Official University of Belgian Congo and Ruanda-Urundi, its replacement by the Katanga State University College and the banning of most of the professors of the former university because they belonged to another Belgian university than that of the adviser of the Katanga Government.[1] Even learning was mixed up in the general disorder which spread through the Congo in the weeks preceding Independence. *The black man saw that the white man's wisdom no longer existed.*

Meanwhile the unrest continued to increase and terrible prophecies circulated—that white estates were to be plundered, white women raped and white men massacred; the terror was growing and by the end of June 1960 the Europeans were in such a state of psychological tension that general panic was to be feared at the first incident. This did not escape the Africans; they understood that henceforth *the white man could no longer protect the black man*, and consequently he could no longer inspire confidence.

Erring Acculturation

Throughout this disorder, and because of it, a characteristic cultural phenomenon appeared which put the finishing touch to the anarchy—a phenomenon known as 'erring acculturation'.

[1] *Pourquoi Pas?*, 11 November; *Le Soir*, 15 November 1960.

We know that acculturation is the effect of contact between two cultures on either of them. Acculturation is directed toward a fairly well defined object, the harmonious adaptation to each other of two or more cultures in contact or of one particular culture to the surrounding changing world. The normal mechanics of acculturation consists in the substitution of a cultural trait or an institution of one culture for that of another. There is acculturation between Western cultures as well as between Western and exotic civilisations, but while in the first case the changes occur gradually and steadily, in the second case we witness something much more rapid—the precipitation, we could even say the catapulting, of Western cultural traits and institutions into an exotic civilisation.

The normal process of acculturation is achieved when the new cultural trait or institution inserts itself harmoniously into the existing culture pattern without causing any trouble; that is the case when the substitution of a new cultural trait for the old one is justified because it responds better to the needs of the society or when its addition to the cultural pattern responds to new needs.

There has always been acculturation on these lines in Africa and there are many examples of culture changes which occurred in tribal societies before the arrival of the Europeans, in order to ensure a better adaptation to new conditions or to new contingencies, such as an invasion, when the invaded had to accept certain of the invaders' political and social institutions, in order to establish normal friendly relations.

When the Europeans penetrated into Africa, a similar process took place according to the same laws. Sometimes acculturation was spontaneous, because the Africans wanted the change; in other cases it was imposed by the European rulers. In both cases acculturation could be accomplished harmoniously and respond to existing needs.

Sometimes, too, acculturation takes place capriciously, without any need or any clearly determined aim; in that case we speak of 'erring acculturation'. The normal process of acculturation is very often accompanied by such capricious changes, but in so far as they remain of secondary importance, and the general trend of development continues logically and involves a constant improvement for the society, no evil will result. Danger appears when erring acculturation dominates.

For years acculturation took place in the Congo in a harmonious way and all efforts went toward the establishment of a balanced African society. A system of local government and traditional courts based upon the tribal units, the stabilisation of labour on the mines, the steady increase of African incomes and the appearance of an African middle class, the improvement of housing, health, education and labour conditions, the gradual abolition of the colour bar, the integration of Africans into an elaborate labour organisation and into advisory boards and councils —all this directed the acculturation of the Congolese and minimised the danger of erring. There was a certain amount of erring in that period and there are many examples of clumsy, although sincere, attempts to incorporate the Western world, and all the things it brought, into the old cosmology: certain magico-religious sects and certain social clubs like the *Ase Belge* in the Northern Sankuru area[1] were typical of that outlook; in fact they tried to approach 'the new world with means and tactics borrowed from the old', i.e. with all those methods which can be covered by the elastic, comfortable term 'magico-religious'.[2]

In certain cases, however, the European administration introduced erring elements into the new African culture pattern, for instance the civic merit card and the immatriculation, which were created in 1948 and 1949 to stimulate

[1] The *Ase Belge* (the Belgians) was an imitation of European society with its whole hierarchy, its whole structure and way of life. Being regarded as contrary to public order, it was forbidden by an Ordinance of 18 July 1941 of the Provincial Governor of Lusambo.

[2] Dr. J. van Baal, 'Erring Acculturation', *American Anthropologist*, vol. 62 no. 1, February 1960, pp. 108–121.

the Congolese towards a better—i.e. a European and Christian-orientated—way of life and should have given them certain rights of assimilation, i.e. made them the equals of the white people. If on paper the effects of these institutions looked sound, in practice they made no change in the subordinate situation of the Africans; thus well-meant institutions contributed to a great disillusionment, to ill-feeling and the frustration of their desire for better things, a frustration which gave birth to envy and distrust.

The very realistic policy of the years 1954 to 1958 emphasised the fact that advancement in wealth and social standing depends on education and professional efficiency; the extension of education, a pre-established programme of wage-increases which doubled the amounts over five years, and many other social improvements gave the Congolese some confidence that better living could be obtained by rational methods.

But this confidence disappeared in 1958 when social progress was halted because of the economic recession, when unemployment increased and thousands of young boys saw themselves debarred from future progress because they could not find a job and there was no room for them in the schools.

It was about that time that Minister Petillon, instead of taking concrete measures to face at once the real problems of the moment, announced with a flourish his policy of 'decolonisation'. If he thought that this abstract and vague conception would galvanise disillusioned Africans, he was wrong, because the word 'independence' appeared at the same time in the African settlements and was immediately surrounded by an aureole of magic.

'Independence' was the miracle word which would give to the Congolese all they were longing for, especially equality of power, knowledge, wealth and social standing with the Europeans. It became a slogan which was thrown in the face of European motorists driving through African settlements, it was written up on walls, songs were sung about it, it was the favourite refrain of all political argument, and it was above all the war-cry of the riots of January 1959 in Leopoldville.

Many Congolese did not grasp the implications of 'independence'; they only understood that they would live in the houses of the Europeans, drive their cars and marry their women, and several paid high amounts to swindlers who promised them these 'goods' on Independence Day. Because their greatest desire was to partake fully in Western ways of life, these people showed themselves blind to the rational sequence of events; they expected miracles to be within their grasp.

Dr. van Baal gave an explanation of this phenomenon, describing similar situations in New Guinea and Melanesia:[1]

'Where wealth and progress figure so obviously in the realm of myth and miracle, it is no wonder that people are induced by the poor outcome of their effort to shut their eyes to the logical sequence of things and concentrate on the realisation of miracles, thus blocking their way to real progress. Repeated failures to realise the coveted miracle do not result in a better understanding of the natural order. The cause of failure is never sought in a misinterpretation of that order but unfailingly in the methods applied to enforce the revelation of the miracle. The belief in miracles allows an endless variation of method in approaching the supernatural. Meanwhile, desire, stimulated where contact is intensified by an increasing display of unattainable wealth, is more and more frustrated by repeated disappointment and ultimately breeds nothing but pure envy.'

Finding no solution to their problems, some exasperated youngsters, after Independence, advocated a return to the conditions that prevailed before the arrival of the Europeans, and even resorted to forms of violence from the ancestral ethos; the *Jeunesses Baluba* of North Katanga resuscitated their ancient war-magicians and revived the use of ritual murder; one of their great chiefs, Kabongo, was killed by them in the same way that pretender-emperors were put to death in the old days; Kabongo's

[1] Van Baal, 'Erring Acculturation', p. 111.

crime was to have disagreed with the spirit of violence of these young people.

Thus erring acculturation, based on distrust of the surrounding world, destroyed in July 1960 the last spark of hope of the Congo reaching Independence in peace and order.

Conclusion

This account is far from complete. I purposely abstained from writing about the tragic events which occurred in the Congo during the last months, because too many details are still missing.

It is not too early, however, to start seeking the causes of these events and to show the motivations of the 'Congo revolution' in their true light, in the hope that the responsible authorities may perhaps take notice of them in their future relations with the Congo Republic.

Perhaps this account could also be useful to the colonial governments of neighbouring African territories which are still dependent, and teach them that they could avoid 'erring acculturation' by facing persistently and courageously, in a realistic, concrete, progressive and constructive way, the problems of the populations they administer.

I will finish with a word of hope. The Congo remains one of the wealthiest nations of 'Black Africa' and its economic possibilities are unlimited. It is marked out for a brilliant future and, in better circumstances, it could have taken a prominent part in African affairs, starting from the first days of its independent existence. Insufficiently prepared for its task, because of a too rapid and badly organised approach to Independence, the Congo will first have to go through its present crisis, which may take some months, if not some years. Nevertheless I remain convinced, and I hope with reason, that African common sense, which I experienced for twenty-four years, will prevail again in the near future. Then, I am sure, the Congo will be able to take up the leadership in Africa for which it is destined.

Table I

Comparative Statistics of Non-European Students in Metropolitan Primary Schools (1956 to 1959)

Racial Groupings	School Years	State-administered (*)	Administered by Religious Bodies		Totals
			on behalf of the State (†)	with State subsidies (**)	
Asians	1956	76	10	113	199
	1957	220	6	43	269
	1958	206	7	58	271
	1959	181	10	70	261
Recognised Eurafricans	1956	104	22	186	312
	1957	126	21	216	363
	1958	151	36	195	382
	1959	174	35	228	437
Non-recognised Eurafricans	1956	46	1	39	85
	1957	61	1	41	103
	1958	52	—	38	90
	1959	62	4	49	115
Africans	1956	162	7	34	203
	1957	176	21	249	446
	1958	379	59	412	850
	1959	682	63	748	1,493
Totals	1956	388	39	372	799
	1957	583	49	549	1,181
	1958	788	102	703	1,593
	1959	1,109	112	1,085	2,306

(*) The State-administered schools were run by a staff appointed directly by the Government and in Government-owned buildings.

(†) In the schools which were administered by religious bodies, on behalf of the State, these religious bodies selected their own teaching staff, which had however to be approved by the Government, which paid the salaries directly to the teachers. The buildings were owned by the Government, but were put at the disposal of the managing religious bodies.

(**) In the schools which were only subsidised by the Government, the teaching staff was likewise selected by the religious bodies, and approved by the State. The teachers received their salaries from the religious body, which was reimbursed by the Government up to eighty per cent. The buildings, which belonged to the religious body, were also subsidised by the Government up to eighty per cent of their value at the time of construction.

TABLE II 89

Table II

CONGOLESE ADMINISTRATIVE STRUCTURE

COLONIAL STRUCTURE *A PROPOSAL FOR A NEW STRUCTURE*
(suggested in 1956)

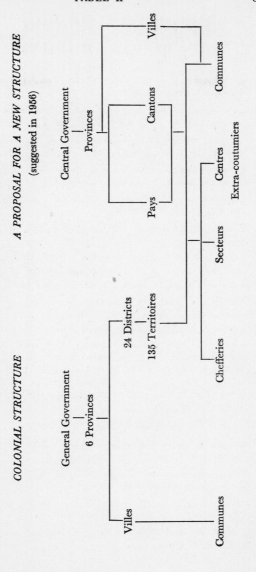

BIBLIOGRAPHY

Artigue, Pierre. *Qui sont les leaders congolais?* (Brussels, Editions Europe-Afrique, 1960).

Brausch, Georges. 'The Problem of Elites in the Belgian Congo', *International Social Science Bulletin*, vol. viii, no. 3, 1956.

— 'Origines de la politique indigène belge en Afrique', *Revue de l'Institut de Sociologie Solvay*, 1955, no. 3, pp. 455–478.

— 'Le paternalisme, une doctrine belge de politique indigène', *Revue de l'Institut de Sociologie Solvay*, 1957, no. 2, pp. 191–217.

— 'Construction d'une nation africaine', *Synthèses*, 11th year, no. 121 (June 1956).

— 'Communes africaines', *Revue de l'Université de Bruxelles*, 9th year (January–April 1957), pp. 230–59.

— 'Pluralisme ethnique et culturel au Congo Belge', *Report of the 30th Session of the International Institute of Differing Civilisations* (INCIDI), held in Lisbon, April 1957, pp. 243–267.

— 'The Solvay Institute of Sociology in Belgian Africa', *International Social Science Journal*, vol. xi, no. 2.

— 'Applied Anthropology in the Belgian Territories in Africa (An Experience of Integration of the Tribal Institutions into the Pattern of the New Social Action in Central Africa)', Selected Papers of the *Fifth International Congress of Anthropological and Ethnological Sciences* (Philadelphia, September 1–9, 1956), University of Pennsylvania Press, Philadelphia, 1960, pp. 755–63.

Calder, Ritchie. *Agony of the Congo* (London, Gollancz, 1961).

Chomé, Jules. *Le drame de Luluabourg* (Brussels, Editions de Remarques Congolaises, 1959).

— *Indépendance congolaise. Pacifique conquête* (Brussels, Editions de Remarques Congolaises, 1960).

— *La crise congolaise* (Brussels, Editions de Remarques Congolaises, 1961).

Congo 1959. Documents belges et africains (Brussels, Les Dossiers du C.R.I.S.P., 1960).

Davister, Pierre. *Katanga, enjeu du monde* (Brussels, Editions Europe–Afrique, 1960).

European Common Market, *Rapport sur la situation sociale dans les pays d'outre-mer associés à la Communauté Economique Européenne* (Brussels, 1960).

Ganshof van der Meersch, W.C. *Congo, mai–juin 1960. Rapport du Ministre Chargé des Affaires Générales en Afrique* (Brussels, 1960).

International Labour Office. *African Labour Survey* (Geneva, 1958).

International Labour Office. *Rapport sur les salaires dans la République du Congo* (Geneva, 1960).

Legum, Colin. *Congo Disaster* (London, Penguin Books, 1961).

Lumumba, Patrice. *Le Congo, terre d'avenir, est-il menacé?* (Brussels, Editions de l'Office de Publicité, 1961).

Pirlot, Yvette. *Une expérience d'action sociale dans un milieu urbain du Congo Belge* (duplicated by the Solvay Katanga Centre of Social Research, 1959).

Problèmes d'Afrique Centrale (Director, Louis Dekoster), Three-monthly Bulletin of the Association des Anciens Etudiants de l'Institut Universitaire des Territoires d'Outre-Mer.

Remarques Congolaises, weekly bulletin of information and documentation (Brussels).

Rubbens, Antoine, and others. *Dettes de guerre* (Elisabethville, Les Cahiers de la Politique Indigène, 1945).

Sepulchre, Jean. *Propos sur le Congo politique de demain. Autonomie et fédéralisme* (Elisabethville, Editions de l'Essor du Congo, 1958).

Slade, Ruth. *The Belgian Congo: Some Recent Changes* (London, Oxford University Press for the Institute of Race Relations, 1960).

Synthèses, no. 121, June 1956 (special issue on the Congo).

Synthèses, nos. 163-4, December 1959—January 1960 (special issue on the Congo).

Van Baal, J. 'Erring acculturation', *American Anthropologist*, vol. 62, no. 1, February 1960, pp. 108–121.

Van Bilsen, A. A. J. 'Un plan de trente ans pour l'émancipation de l'Afrique belge', *Les Dossiers de l'Action Sociale Catholique*, Brussels, 33rd year, no. 2 (February 1956), pp. 83–111.

Van Langenhove, Fernand. *Consciences tribales et nationales en Afrique Noire* (The Hague, Martinus Nijhoff, 1960).

— 'La crise congolaise: 1 janvier 1959–15 août 1960', *Chronique de Politique Etrangère* (Institut Royal des Relations Internationales), vol. xiii, nos. 4–6 (July–November 1960).

Van Reyn, Paul. *Le Congo politique: les partis et les élections* (Brussels, Editions Europe-Afrique, 1960).

Vermeulen, V. *Déficiences et dangers de notre politique indigène* (Imprimerie I.M.A., 1953).